Hearers to Kneelers to Chosen

The Transformed Life

Cycle B Second Lesson Sermons for Advent, Christmas, and Epiphany

Ron Love

CSS Publishing Company, Inc.
Lima, Ohio

Hearers to Kneelers to Chosen
The Transformed Life
Cycle B Second Lesson Sermons for
Advent, Christmas, and Epiphany

FIRST EDITION
Copyright © 2017
by CSS Publishing Co., Inc.

Published by CSS Publishing Company, Inc., Lima, Ohio 45807. All rights reserved. No part of this publication may be reproduced in any manner whatsoever without the prior permission of the publisher, except in the case of brief quotations embodied in critical articles and reviews. Inquiries should be addressed to: CSS Publishing Company, Inc., Permissions Department, 5450 N. Dixie Highway, Lima, Ohio 45807.

Library of Congress Cataloging-in-Publication Data
Names: Love, Ronald H., author.
Title: Hearers to kneelers to chosen : the transformed life : Cycle B second lesson sermons for Advent, Christmas, and Epiphany / Ron Love.
Description: FIRST EDITION. | Lima, Ohio : CSS Publishing Company, Inc., 2017. | Includes bibliographical references and index.
Identifiers: LCCN 2017027449 (print) | LCCN 2017036283 (ebook) | ISBN 9780788028922 (eBook) | ISBN 0788028928 (eBook) | ISBN 780788028908 (pbk. : alk. paper) | ISBN 0788028901 (pbk. : alk. paper)
Subjects: LCSH: Advent sermons. | Christmas sermons. | Epiphany--Sermons. | Bible. New Testament--Sermons. | Common lectionary (1992). Year B.
Classification: LCC BV4254.5 (ebook) | LCC BV4254.5 .L68 2017 (print) | DDC 252/.61--dc23

For more information about CSS Publishing Company resources, visit our website at www.csspub.com, email us at csr@csspub.com, or call (800) 241-4056.

e-book:
ISBN-13: 978-0-7880-2892-2
ISBN-10: 0-7880-2892-8

ISBN-13: 978-0-7880-2890-8
ISBN-10: 0-7880-2890-1   PRINTED IN USA

*To my Mother — The most angelic person, who sings poetic with
the Christmas angels of Bethlehem.*

Table of Contents

Advent 1 1 Corinthians 1:3-9 "Cathedra"	7
Advent 2 2 Peter 3:8-15a Wavering Notes by an Uncertain Trumpet	13
Advent 3 1 Thessalonians 5:16-24 Standing in the Forecastle	21
Advent 4 Romans 16:25-27 Soli Deo Gloria	28
Christmas Eve / Day Titus 2:11-14 In diem natalem	34
Christmas 1 Galatians 4:4-7 Abba! Father!	41
Epiphany Day Ephesians 3:1-12 The Foot-board of the Pulpit and the Floor of the Parlor	48
Epiphany 2 1 Corinthians 6:12-20 Our Magic Mirror	55
Epiphany 3 1 Corinthians 7:29-31 Undivided Attention	62

Epiphany 4   69
1 Corinthians 8:1-13
I Hope It Helped

Epiphany 5   76
1 Corinthians 9:16-23
140 or 300,000

Transfiguration of Our Lord   83
2 Corinthians 4:3-6
The Red Coat

Advent 1
1 Corinthians 1:3-9

"Cathedra"

Grace to you and peace from God our Father and the Lord Jesus Christ. I give thanks to my God always for you because of the grace of God that has been given you in Christ Jesus, for in every way you have been enriched in him, in speech and knowledge of every kind — just as the testimony of Christ has been strengthened among you — so that you are not lacking in any spiritual gift as you wait for the revealing of our Lord Jesus Christ. He will also strengthen you to the end, so that you may be blameless on the day of our Lord Jesus Christ. God is faithful; by him you were called into the fellowship of his son, Jesus Christ our Lord.
1 Corinthians 1:3-9

  He sat quietly in the pew to the left of the altar at St. John's Anglican Church in Richmond, Virginia. Having been elected to the House of Burgesses from Howard County just nine days earlier, he was hesitant to speak publicly. Especially when seated around him were such distinguished men as George Washington, Thomas Jefferson, and James Madison. The delegates were in debate and divided on how to respond to the Stamp Act that had been imposed upon the colonies by England. The Stamp Act was a British law that placed a tax on printed documents in the colonies. As proof of paying the tax, each document had to have an authorized stamp. The debate was centered on compliance or severing the colonies' relationship with the England.
  On Thursday, March 23, 1775, having sat quietly long enough, Patrick Henry stood where he was seated. Speaking without notes, and in a voice that increasing became louder and more empathic,

he advocated raising a militia and declaring independence from the King of England.

The climax of the speech was the closing line that has become a hallmark of American patriotism when Henry declared, "Forbid it, almighty God! I know not what course others may take; but as for me, give me liberty, or give me death!"

Patrick Henry's oration brought unity to the delegates attending the Virginia Provincial Convention. In the days following Patrick Henry's speech, the delegates passed all seven resolutions declaring their independence from England.

It is easier to sit quietly than it is to stand and speak. This is especially the case when we realize that there are others who are more eloquent speakers and more knowledgeable speakers than you or I may be. But, there does come a time when we must rise up from our pew and speak.

Public speaking can take on many forms. It can be as dramatic as standing forthright in one's pew, left of center of the pulpit, and in words that are unmistakably loud enough for everyone to hear as we present our position. Public speaking can come in a less dramatic format, as when we share our thoughts in a small group setting. This can be in a Sunday school class, a home Bible study group, or among a gathering of friends in a social setting. Public speaking can also be private speaking as we share out thoughts with just one other person.

But, speak we must. We are comfortable speaking on many topics ranging from our occupations to our hobbies to our families and to current events. But, there is one topic that we are uncomfortable with and that is sharing our Christian faith. But, this is one topic that we can never avoid discussing with others. We must be willing and prepared to tell others about Jesus Christ and what Jesus means in our own lives. We are called to be witnesses of the gospel message and this is a calling that we cannot forsake.

Our lectionary reading for this morning is Paul's introduction to his letter to the church in Corinth. He begins with his standard greeting writing, "Grace to you and peace from God our Father and the Lord Jesus Christ." And then, as it is Paul's custom, he thanks those who are serving the church.

Then Paul in his opening paragraph does something a little different from some of his other letters. Paul gives a brief outline of what he is going to discuss in the following pages. The central problem that Paul is going to discuss is the disunity among the members of the Corinthian church. Paul is concerned that some of those who are speaking publicly are not preaching the gospel message that he has taught them. In the Corinthian church, there are several speakers with differing gospel messages that is causing confusion and havoc among the parishioners. Paul wants all of those who are speaking to share the message that Paul taught them without any deviation.

As Patrick Henry standing to the left side of the sanctuary brought unity and harmony to the Virginia Provincial Convention, it is time once again for those in this sanctuary to hear one message, to receive one direction, and to follow one course of action. We have a single message, because as Paul understood it, we are gathered for the sake of unity and having a common purpose and direction.

Paul, in our lesson this morning, highlighted that the church is a community and those in the community have varying spiritual gifts that can be used for the enrichment of everyone. But, of those spiritual gifts Paul makes special note of two — speech and knowledge. This again is because some of those who are speaking are not sharing what Paul taught them, so the congregation is not only hearing conflicting messages, but some of the messages are wrong.

This brings Paul to his other point, which is that those who are speaking must have knowledge. Those who are speaking must be knowledgeable of the Christian message. And for Paul that means sharing what Paul taught them when he was living among them.

One of the reasons, and maybe the main reason, why we are hesitant to speak is our fear of having a lack of an adequate understanding of the Bible and religion.

We can learn of the importance of Christian education from the early church. The postapostolic church took the mandate for Christian education very seriously. The postapostolic church spanned the first four centuries of the history of the church.

During the postapostolic period, each bishop held a teaching chair, called a "cathedra." Therefore, the building in which the bishop resided was called a "cathedral." Within the cathedral was an "episcopal school." It was an episcopal school because the bishop was the primary instructor. The region over which the bishop presided came to be called an "episcopate." It was to these episcopal schools that the elders of the church who came from the episcopate, that is, from the congregations for which the bishop was responsible, came for instruction. The elders would then return to their congregations located within the episcopate to instruct others.

The elders in the community churches would accept the responsibility of educating new converts. The sole purpose of this instruction was preparation for baptism. Once baptized the formal education ceased. The method of instruction was dialogue and memorization, as most students were illiterate and written materials were scarce. The participants studied the creeds and liturgies of the church, in addition to the bishop's approved list of apostolic writings. Apostolic writings are the writings, or the teachings, of the recognized leaders of the church.

The period of instruction lasted two to three years, with three grades or classes of catechumens. When first admitted, they were called "hearers," for they listened to instruction and sermons. The next grade was "kneelers," for they remained for the prayers after the hearers withdrew. Also, further advance instruction was also provided to the kneelers. The final class was called "the chosen." These catechumens were given intense doctrinal instruction because the elders had to be sure that the new converts would not recant when confronted with martyrdom. Thus, they were known as "the chosen" for the elders of the church found them worthy to be chosen to be baptized into the Christian faith.

Hearers, kneelers, chosen — perhaps this concept ought to be incorporated into our confirmation classes today. And for those of us beyond the age of attending confirmation class, perhaps this concept ought to be incorporated into our lives as well.

What the three-stage process of hearers, kneelers, and chosen really means is to have a serious and disciplined approach to learning the message of Jesus. It means to have an overwhelming desire to be knowledgeable of the scriptures. When we have confidence in having obtained this knowledge, we will be less hesitant to speak about Jesus both publicly and privately.

In this process of becoming knowledgeable of the scriptures our church is a form of a cathedral, or learning center. We may not be a massive stone structure with an overpowering stone bell tower at our entrance, and majestic stone columns in our sanctuary, with a cobble stone aisle flanked by hand carved oak pews; but nonetheless, we are the seat of Christian learning in our community today. For within these walls of made of stucco are multiple opportunities for learning.

We should not discard the sermon as only a message of inspiration, for it is also a message of spiritual enlightenment. There are Sunday school classes to attend that provide a formal presentation with a chance for dialogue. During the course of the year we offer some special seminars. Being engaged in the administration of the church and participating in the ministry projects of the church is also an educational experience. It goes without saying that it is important to have our children in Sunday school and our youth involved in our evening programs. If you afford yourselves of the opportunities present in this cathedral you can, over the years, make the transition in your own spiritual lives from hearers to kneelers to being the chosen.

Your home can become its own cathedral, or learning center. If you take time to read the Bible each day, pray, read devotional literature, and read thought provoking books by good Christian authors. If you engage yourself in these daily spiritual exercises you will become a more knowledgeable Christian.

It is with this knowledge that you will become a more confident speaker. That is why Paul in his letter wrote, "For in every way you have been enriched in him, in speech and knowledge of every kind."

Norman Vincent Peale was the pastor of Marble Collegiate Church in New York City for 52 years. It is the church that our current president, Donald Trump, attended when he lived in New York. Peale is probably better known for his book *The Power of Positive Thinking* that was published in 1952. The book was part theology and part psychology as it emphasized the importance of being optimistic. It was an optimism that was based on having faith in Jesus and believing in the promises of Jesus.

Peale grew up in Lynchburg, Ohio. His father was a Methodist minister. As a child, he attended a Sunday school class taught by his mother. One day she began a lesson describing the stamina of the Cincinnati Reds, baseball players who were the heroes to all the boys in the class. Then she launched into a description of Jesus and how Jesus "set his face to go to Jerusalem" knowing well the fate that awaited him. Mother, as Peale recited, called it "guts." At that young age, Peale came to realize this of Jesus: "What courage!" "What a man!"

Norman Vincent Peale by attending Sunday school learned about Jesus, a man of courage. And with that knowledge Peale became a courageous speaker. In fact, Peale became one of the most sought after speakers in the mid-twentieth century. Even more so, Peale became the educator and an inspiration of a future president.

You and I will never stand in the pulpit of Marble Collegiate Church. You and I will never have a future president as a Sunday school student. But each of us does have the calling of Paul that we are to speak, and when we speak we are to speak with knowledge.

Amen.

Advent 2
2 Peter 3:8-15a

Wavering Notes by an Uncertain Trumpet

But do not ignore this one fact, beloved, that with the Lord one day is like a thousand years, and a thousand years are like one day. The Lord is not slow about his promise, as some think of slowness, but is patient with you, not wanting any to perish, but all to come to repentance. But the day of the Lord will come like a thief, and then the heavens will pass away with a loud noise, and the elements will be dissolved with fire, and the earth and everything that is done on it will be disclosed. Since all these things are to be dissolved in this way, what sort of persons ought you to be in leading lives of holiness and godliness, waiting for and hastening the coming of the day of God, because of which the heavens will be set ablaze and dissolved, and the elements will melt with fire? But, in accordance with his promise, we wait for new heavens and a new earth, where righteousness is at home. Therefore, beloved, while you are waiting for these things, strive to be found by him at peace, without spot or blemish; and regard the patience of our Lord as salvation. So also our beloved brother Paul wrote to you according to the wisdom given him.
2 Peter 3:8-15a

Benjamin Gilman served in the United States House of Representatives for thirty years. He retired from Congress in 2003. Gilman represented New York's 27th congressional district. Gilman served as the chair of the House Committee on Foreign Affairs, and he was the congressional reprehensive to the United Nations. Gilman, a Republican, was an outspoken critic of President Bill Clinton's foreign policy. He especially disapproved of the favoritism that Clinton showed Russia over the former Soviet Republics that were able to gain their independence. Addressing the Clinton foreign policy Gilman said, "Instead of a strong, steady signal on foreign policy coming from the nation's capital, regrettably the world has heard a series of wavering notes by an uncertain trumpet, leaving our allies concerned, and our adversaries confused."

Wavering notes by an uncertain trumpet instead of a strong and steady signal. This can only leave people concerned, as well as confused.

Wavering notes by an uncertain trumpet is the issue that Peter addresses in our lectionary reading this morning. Peter wrote this letter shortly before his death, and he sent the letter to the various churches in Asia Minor. The letter was written sometime between the year 65 and the year 68.

The wavering notes from an uncertain trumpet that Peter addressed are the false teachers who were preaching a message that contradicted everything that Peter had taught. Peter emphasized in the letter that he knew Jesus personally and was a witness to the ministry and teaching of Jesus. Parishioners need to stop listening to wavering notes form an uncertain trumpet, that is the message of false teachers, and return to listening to the strong and steady message that Peter proclaimed.

The first-century church expected the immediate return of Jesus in their life time. They believed that the second coming would actually occur before their death.

The apostle Paul was a firm believer in this, which influenced his position on social issues. For example, Paul wrote to the church in Corinth, "Are you free from a wife? Do not seek marriage." Paul understood that a married man could not fully devote himself to preaching the gospel message. And since Jesus is going to return within Paul's lifetime, having a wife would prevent a man from being fully dedicated to the task of evangelism. Since Jesus was coming soon, within the next few years or at the latest in the next decade, anything that kept a man from the imperative of evangelism, which would include marriage, must be forsaken to preach the message of salvation.

Today we realize that even though there is an urgency to preach the gospel message, we do not have to forsake marriage to do so.

The problem that Peter confronted was that it had been over thirty years and Jesus had not returned. This led the false teachers to preach a message that Jesus was not going to return. The uncertain trumpets with wavering notes gave several arguments that what Peter believed, what Paul believed, and what the other apostles believed about the immediate return of Jesus was a misguided doctrine.

Eugene Boring, a contemporary scholar of our time, is a New Testament professor at Brite Divinity School, located on the campus of Texas Christian University. Boring is the author of many respected books on the New Testament. In a commentary on Second Peter he offers three reasons why some Christian teachers held the position that Christ was not going to return in the near future.

First, the false teachers taught that since Jesus did not return within the expected time, history had shown it to be a false expectation.

Second, the false teachers taught the constancy and consistency of world order, that it continued to function as it always had, showing that history would continue without divine intervention — hence there was no final judgment to be feared.

Third, the false teachers taught that since Christ had set us free from following the laws of Judaism we would not be called into account for our actions. For this reason, judgment was unnecessary.

The arguments presented by Boring described the false teachers as saying that since nothing seemed to have changed since the resurrection of Jesus, and since it seemed nothing would change, we were free from the final judgment. The false teachers were saying that since Jesus had not returned immediately as was expected, Jesus was not going to return, so we could continue as we always had since there was no fear of a final judgment.

Peter was up against an audience that believed it was okay to continue to live a life of the flesh, a life of fulfilling earthly desires; rather than to live a life of the Spirit, a life that fulfills God's heavenly desires.

Peter addressed these false teachers by writing that we must be "patient." Just because God had not intervened in human history as we expected God to do; we needed to be patient, we needed the ability to patiently wait for God to thunder forth as promised.

John Ruskin once said, "Endurance is nobler than strength, and patience than beauty." Ruskin was born in London in 1819. As an adult, he continued in the family business as wine merchant, which made him very wealthy. As a child, his father interested John in art, and his pious Protestant mother created an interest in John to study the Bible. As a merchant, Ruskin travelled to many countries, and in each country, he took the time to study art of the native land. As a Bible scholar, he took time to learn about the people in each country he did business in. From these two perspectives, he wrote a number of books that interpreted the great paintings through history. Perhaps this is why Ruskin considered patience as a form of beauty. Again, I will repeat the quote, John Ruskin said, "Endurance is nobler than strength and patience than beauty."

We probably don't associate patience with beauty. We usually think of patience as something being forced upon us because we cannot have what we want now, this day, this moment. Patience for us is usually accompanied by anxiety, frustration, and a sense of helplessness. Certainly, this does not describe patience as being beautiful.

But perhaps patience can be beautiful if we take a different perspective of it. *Dictionary.com* has an interesting definition of patience describing it as a "quiet, steady perseverance; even tempered care; diligence." Listen to those words again and see the beauty that Ruskin saw in patience, as patience is a "quiet, steady perseverant; even tempered careful; diligent."

Peter was trying to tell the church members across Asia Minor that they should not listen to the false teachers, but be patient. Peter realized there was a beauty in patience that gave one the noble qualities of being "quiet, steady perseverance; even tempered care; diligence."

An impatient person for Peter is one who lives an immoral life because Jesus has not returned and therefore concludes there is no final judgment. An impatient person for Peter is one who believes that there is no final accounting for how one has lived.

Instead, a patient person lives a quiet, diligent life of perseverance knowing Christ will return, and that there will be a final judgment. A diligent life is not one that ignores the commandments of Jesus, but a diligent person patiently waits while remaining obedient to the scriptures.

It is now the year 2017. It has now been 1,984 years since the resurrection of Jesus. After almost 2,000 years the question is this — can we still remain patient and obedient to the scriptures; or, will we say there is no use in waiting and there will be no final judgment so I am going to live by my own fleshly desires?

The false teachers argued that since everything is the same after several decades since the resurrection there is no final judgment, you can live as you like. But Jesus said, as recorded in Matthew's gospel, "As it was in the days of Noah, so it will be at the coming of the Son of Man. For in the days before the flood, people were eating and drinking, marrying and giving in marriage, up to the day Noah entered the ark."

Yes, Jesus did say that on the day of the second coming everything will seem normal. Because of this normalcy the false teachers said that Jesus will not return, and that there will be no final judgment. But Peter is trying to reeducate the parishioners to remain patient and obedient because as normal as things may seem today, Jesus is going to thunder forth on a fiery chariot in judgment.

It is this normalcy that causes us to be lax in following the commandments of Jesus. I know we all talk about the second coming, but I often wonder how serious people really are about it. Since it has been almost 2,000 years and everything still appears normal do we really expect Jesus to descend from heaven in our lifetime? Those who lived in the age of Noah did not believe it. The false teachers did not believe it. Jesus believed it, but do we? And if we believe it, do we live our lives accordingly?

Do we believe in the real possibility of the immediate return of Jesus? As we strolled up the sidewalk into church this morning we looked at traffic going down the street as normal as ever, we saw the blue sky is tranquil as ever, the trees are as majestic as ever, the gentle wind is crisp and refreshing as ever; so, do we really believe that the sky is going to suddenly open, and we will hear angels singing the hallelujah chorus, and we will see Christ seated upon the throne, and then we will instantly realize that judgment is upon us? With a sickening feeling in our stomachs and a look of horror on our faces, we will realize that now, this day, as it was in the days of Noah, it will be too late for us to get on board the ark.

We talk about the second coming, but do we really consider it to be a realistic message? And if we do think of it as a realistic message everything seems so pristine this morning we know it won't happen today. In fact, since history seems to be uninterrupted as the false teachers taught, do we even think it will happen during our lifespan?

The false teachers did not think it would happen. Peter was certain that it will happen.

To help put patience into perspective, Peter wrote a line that I think most everyone has memorized. Peter wrote, "That with the Lord one day is like a thousand years, and a thousand years are like one day." We have inappropriately applied this verse to everything but what Peter intended. We have used it to try to justify the seven days of creation, saying those seven days are not like our seven days today. We have used it to give a reason for unanswered prayer, that God's time in answering prayer is not the same as our time. The list could be extended for several more minutes.

Peter understood "that with the Lord one day is like a thousand years, and a thousand years are like one day" is a confession that God's concept of time is not contained within our human perspective of time. It is a confession that we cannot understand the mysteries of God. If we cannot understand the mysteries of God as it relates to time, then we must have patience.

And patience, remember, is beautiful. Patience is beautiful, as patience is a quiet steady perseverance. The message of quiet steady perseverance is what Peter wants to instill in those who hear his letter read during worship. As congregations were illiterate and every letter had to be reproduced by hand, the letters were only made available to the Christian populace as they were read from the pulpit.

We wait for the second coming with a patience that is beautiful for it is a quiet steady perseverance. Remember, that Peter is addressing his letter to Christians who have fallen under the shadow of false teachers who said Jesus was not returning. False teachers who said since Jesus was not returning there was no final judgment. False teachers who said in the absence of Jesus' returning and no final judgment, we can live the debaucherous lifestyle we have always embraced.

Peter feared, correctly, that those who followed these false teachers would no longer live a Christian life-style. They would become morally lax. The flesh would take precedence over the Spirit.

Peter wrote that as we wait patiently we are to "strive to be found by Jesus at peace, without spot or blemish." We are to continue to live in the image of Jesus. We are to be obedient to all the teachings in the Sermon on the Mount. We should always keep before us the list of Christian attributes that are recorded by Paul in Galatians. These are: "the fruit of the Spirit is love, joy, peace, forbearance, kindness, goodness, faithfulness, gentleness and self-control."

Paul said Jesus is going to return in final judgment, but until then we are to wait patiently living a life that is reflected as one of love, joy, peace, forbearance, kindness, goodness, faithfulness, gentleness, and self-control.

Let us not forget that *Dictionary.com* also uses the word "diligence" to define patience. This would be in keeping with Peter's understanding of patience; that is, while we wait we must be diligent in our service to the Lord. We must have a purpose, a ministry, and a mission in serving the church and helping others. It is not enough just to have the spirit of love; we must also have the spirit of action. If we are involved while waiting for that day and hour we do not know, it will no longer seem so foreboding.

Count Nicolaus Ludwig von Zinzendorf having completed his studies at Wittenberg in 1720, embarked on a grand tour of the continent. To further his education, it was his ambition to visit all the great cultural institutions. During this expedition, his pilgrimage took him to the art museum in Dusseldorf, Germany. It was here that he was transformed from a man of worldly riches to one of humble service to the poor. It occurred simply enough, by looking into the face of Christ.

The Count was admiring Domenico Feti's painting *Ecco Homo*. This is the Latin translation of words spoken by Pilate as he handed Jesus over for crucifixion. This was when Pilate said to the gathered crowd "Behold the Man." The painting was a portrait of the thorn-crowned Jesus of Nazareth, wearing a dark tattered robe, bound neck and wrist in rope. At the base of the painting was the inscription, "I have done this for you — now what will you do for me?"

The young count was profoundly moved. He felt he was embracing a mystical experience while viewing the painting. Nicolaus felt as if Christ himself was speaking those words directly to his own soul. He vowed that day to dedicate his life to the service of Jesus. Reflecting on the transformation of his character von Zinzendorf wrote, "I have loved him for a long time, but I have never actually done anything for him. From now on I will do whatever he leads me to do." Realizing the insignificance of his life's accomplishments he embarked upon a life of meaning and purpose. Nicolaus Ludwig von Zinzendorf remained true to his promise, establishing the religious group that became known as the Moravians.

All of us must stand beneath Feti's painting *Ecco Homo*, looking into the face of Jesus while asking ourselves: What have I done for Jesus who has done so much for me? How dedicated am I to serve in the name of Christ? How obediently do I adhere to scriptural mandates? How willing have I been to sacrifice my time and service and money for God's glory?

These are the questions we must ask ourselves while we patiently wait in that interim period of "that with the Lord one day is like a thousand years, and a thousand years are like one day."

Amen.

Advent 3
1 Thessalonians 5:16-24

Standing in the Forecastle

Rejoice always, pray without ceasing, give thanks in all circumstances; for this is the will of God in Christ Jesus for you. Do not quench the Spirit. Do not despise the words of prophets, but test everything; hold fast to what is good; abstain from every form of evil. May the God of peace himself sanctify you entirely; and may your spirit and soul and body be kept sound and blameless at the coming of our Lord Jesus Christ. The one who calls you is faithful, and he will do this.
1 Thessalonians 5:16-24

Bob Keeshan entertained children for years as the jovial Captain Kangaroo. The television show *Captain Kangaroo* ran on CBS for nearly thirty years, from October 1955 until December 1984, making it one of the longest-running nationally broadcasted children's television programs.

In Keeshan's autobiography *Growing Up Happy*, he shared the moment when he realized life would be marvelous. Shortly after the Second World War, Keeshan, an eighteen-year-old Marine, was on board the troopship USS Rockbridge Ranger sailing toward his last duty station in Hawaii. He enjoyed spending the dark nights standing in the forecastle, gazing at the starlit skies. The bow dipped into each succeeding wave and when it raised the heavens shown gloriously overhead. Reflecting on this experience Keeshan wrote, "There was a rhythm to life, I felt at those moments. I didn't know what was going to happen to me when I was discharged, but I would be nineteen and I was convinced that the world would be wonderful."

As we approach Christmas we have a feeling of tranquility. We have a feeling that all is right with the world. We have a feeling that the world is wonderful. We have this feeling because of the spirit of Christmas. It is the spirit of Christmas that the coming of the child Jesus will make all things new. It is the spirit of Christmas that the child in the manger will become our comforter and our protector. It is the spirit of Christmas that lets us know our sins will be forgiven and that heaven will be our final resting place.

It is in Christmas season that on the darkest of nights when our problems seem to overwhelm us we can stand in the forecastle, gazing at the starlit skies. When the bow of our lives dips with despair into each succeeding wave of sorrow, when it rises again we will see the heavens shinning gloriously overhead.

The shepherds saw a heavenly chorus of angels among the stars. The three wise men followed a beautiful star. When we look up at the stars we see Christ enthroned in the heavens. Yes, this does convince us that the world is wonderful.

The newspaper comic *Real Life Adventures* discusses the real-life problems we all encounter in the course of the day. The comic addresses the ordinary mundane aspects of life. The everyday chores, squabbles, and quirks of humankind are successfully parodied in the comic. The writers Gary Wise and Lance Aldrich were able to do this in a humorous way, but the power of their message is never lost. In their Christmas comic there was no humor, but only a powerful message to contemplate.

In the Christmas issue of *Real Life Adventures* a father and his son were looking out the window of their home. A Christmas tree could be seen behind them. Outside the window snow was gently falling, and two pine trees were covered with snow. The scene was very heartwarming. The father, with his hand on his son's shoulder, listened to the boy's question, "Whatcha looking at, Dad?" To which his father replied, "Peace on earth."

The world is wonderful. Peace on earth. That is the message of Christmas. That is the message of the church.

In our lectionary reading for this morning, the apostle Paul shares with us the three attributes of a genuine church and all three attributes are reflected in our understanding of Christmas. The three attributes are: a happy church, a praying church, and a thankful church. Happy — praying — thankful. Let us hope we are that church. Let us hope we can become that church.

Each year NBC has a Christmas tradition of broadcasting a live musical. The performance in 2016 was *Hairspray*. But in

2016 NBC made an addition to their live telecast. The addition was that some of the commercials would also be live, not pre-recorded. NBC Entertainment Chairman Bob Greenblatt said of this new endeavor, "The more you can make the audience feel that the ads are a part of the zeitgeist of the show, the less they feel like, 'oh, it's a pharmaceutical ad in the middle of this joyous musical.'"

The proclamation of the birth of the child by the prophets and the angels makes those of us in the congregation feel like we are a part of the celebration. And being a part of the Christmas celebration will make us a happy, praying, and thankful congregation.

Let us first discuss what it means to be a happy church. In a happy church, there is an atmosphere of joy that makes the members of the congregation feel that they are bathed in the Christmas spirit. Parishioners find that being a part of the church is exhilarating, not depressing.

A happy church knows that Jesus is the light of the world. Jesus taught, "I am the light of the world. Whoever follows me will never walk in darkness, but will have the light of life." We won't see darkness if we keep facing Jesus, the light of the world. We must remember, that if we face the sun our shadow will fall behind us; but, if we turn our backs on the sun our shadows will fall in front of us. The message of a happy church is that if we continue to face Jesus, the light of the world, all of our problems will be behind us.

If we follow Jesus we will, in the words of Jesus, "have the light of life." The light of life — isn't that a wonderful description of what it means to be happy? And wouldn't it be wonderful if everyone sitting in our sanctuary felt that this church was for them the light of life? Just think, what if the people in our surrounding community saw our church as the light of life? Would they not be drawn to that light? It would be the light of a happy church.

A happy church exhibits the wholesome spiritual attributes that our presented by Paul which are: "love, joy, peace, forbearance, kindness, goodness, faithfulness, gentleness, and self-control." If everyone in our congregation practiced being loving, joyful, peaceful, kind, and gentle, this would be a happy church.

And how do we become a loving, joyful, peaceful, kind and gentle church? It is by practicing Paul's second attribute of being a genuine church; and that is, by being a praying church.

Francis of Assisi was born in 1181. Francis was born into a very wealthy family, and in that environment, he focused his life on money and glory. Growing up, his father's wealth allowed Francis to live a life of debauchery. In his quest for glory he joined the Fourth Crusades. In his snobbish desire to display his wealth he ordered that a suit of armor be made for him decorated with gold with a magnificent cloak.

But Francis only got one day's ride into the crusade when he had a dream in which God told him he had life all wrong. Francis returned home with an understanding of the meaning of humility and poverty.

The real transformation of his life came when he took some cloth from his father's store to help repair the church in Assai. His father, Pietro Bernardone, had Francis taken before the bishop, demanding that all the money be returned to the store. The bishop told Francis to return the money because God would provide.

That was all Francis needed to hear. He not only gave back the money but stripped off all the clothes his father had given him until he was wearing only a hair shirt. In front of the crowd that had gathered Francis said, "Pietro Bernardone is no longer my father. From now on I can say with complete freedom, 'Our Father who art in heaven.'"

Wearing nothing but castoff rags, he went off into the freezing woods singing. When robbers later beat him and took his clothes, he climbed out of the ditch and went off singing again. In the year 1208, Francis began to preach and slowly gathered a group of followers. This group founded the Franciscan order. The Franciscan order is a monastic group that follows a strict order of prayer and poverty.

Francis' life was changed when he said the Lord's Prayer. Francis was fully converted to Christianity when he could pray "Our Father who art in heaven." It was then that Francis discovered his mission in life. It was then that Francis experienced joy and peace. It was then when Francis became a happy person. It all came when Francis learned how to pray.

Prayer is a relationship, wherein we humbly communicate, worship, and sincerely seek God's face, knowing that God does hear our prayers. Because God loves us God will respond to our prayers, though not always in a manner we may expect or desire. Our prayers can encompass confession, praise, adoration, supplication, and intercession.

In addition to God's response to us, our response to God is important. Our attitude in prayer is important. We must not be haughty, but humble. We must pray continually, which means that we must always strive to have a prayerful attitude. Our prayers must come often and regularly, not from a legalistic duty, but from a humble heart, realizing our dependence on God in every aspect of our lives.

One of the most reassuring things about prayer is that it is always available to us. Nothing can keep us from approaching God in prayer except our own choice not to pray.

As a church we realize that prayer not only strengthens our relationship with God, but when we pray with other believers, prayer also strengthens the bonds between fellow Christians.

Prayer according to Paul is one of the three essential components to a genuine church. As members of this congregation we must accept the obligation to live a prayerful life. We need to have a private prayer life as well as a corporate prayer life. We pray quietly and alone during our time of personal daily meditation. We pray corporately as a congregation in worship and in Sunday school class, and before church meetings.

The blessing of a congregation where individuals pray privately and in groups is that we become a church that is totally focused on God.

Abraham Lincoln, the sixteenth President of the United States, once said, "I have been driven many times upon my knees by the overwhelming conviction that I had nowhere else to go. My own wisdom and that of all about me seemed insufficient for that day."

Prayer is an attribute of a genuine church because we know our earthly wisdom is not sufficient. In prayer, we seek the wisdom and presence of God.

The apostle Paul's third attribute of a genuine church is that it is a thankful church. Christmas is the season of the year when we are most likely to talk about our blessings. Part of this discussion is represented by our gifts, that are so brightly and beautiful wrapped, that are shared with others. Christmas gifts are not a commercialization of Christmas, but a means of expressing our love and bestowing a blessing upon another person.

I know that there are many individuals in the sanctuary this morning where being thankful seems to be the farthest thing from them. Hardships have overtaken many. Some are facing financial distress. Others are experiencing estrangement from a family member. Stress at work has become daunting. Big decisions that must be made during the coming year are overwhelming.

I guess like Mary and Joseph in the stable and with Herod on the throne, things could not seem more bleak. But then, when Mary and Joseph looked into the manger and saw the Christ child, hope and peace was instilled within them. We too must take our eyes off Herod and fix our gaze upon the child in the manger. When we can do that, we will become thankful.

Kermit the Frog, who is that adorable Muppet from the television program *Sesame Street*, once said, "Be thankful for the bad things in life. For they opened your eyes to the good things you weren't paying attention to before!"

This is the season for us to pay attention to the good things in life. For those who are experiencing problems a good thing is the birth of Christ. We tend to focus all of our attention on those problems that infect our lives. But, as Kermit said, we also need to be able to see the good things we have in our lives. It would be good now for everyone seated in the sanctuary to start making a mental list of all your many wonderful and joyful blessings. There are many, and some of those blessings in a few weeks will be gathered about your decorated Christmas tree.

The Ice Bucket Challenge has probably been forgotten by everyone by now. Remember it? You challenged a friend to have a bucket of ice water dumped on their head, and then make a donation to the find a cure for Lou Gehrig's Disease. The 2014 challenge raised $220 million. The person who started it, the Boston College baseball captain, Pete Frates, who had Lou Gehrig's Disease, received the NCAA 2017 Inspirational Award. The award was a way for the basketball community and society at large to say thanks.

Let us leave the sanctuary today dedicating ourselves to being a genuine church. Let us be a happy church, a praying church, a

thankful church.
 Amen.

Advent 4
Romans 16:25-27

Soli Deo Gloria

Now to God who is able to strengthen you according to my gospel and the proclamation of Jesus Christ, according to the revelation of the mystery that was kept secret for long ages but is now disclosed, and through the prophetic writings is made known to all the Gentiles, according to the command of the eternal God, to bring about the obedience of faith — to the only wise God, through Jesus Christ, to whom be the glory forever! Amen.
Romans 16:25-27

    Carol Klein, with schoolbooks under one arm and a sheet of music under the other, got off the express train from Brooklyn to Manhattan. The year was 1957 and the 15-year-old was determined to be a singing sensation. Wearing bobby socks, white sneakers, and a black skirt with a pink poodle embroidered on it, she opened the New York City telephone book. Starting with the "As" in the directory, she visited every music industry executive until she found one who would record her songs.
    After being turned away by several recording studios, ABC-Paramount invited her to record four songs. Five decades later we know her as Carol King who has over twenty solo albums. At the age of 71, King was the first woman, on May 22, 2013, to receive Library of Congress' Gershwin Prize for Popular Song. The award is named after the music-writing team of George and Ira Gershwin.

Whenever King performs at a concert, a large number of Baby Boomers are in attendance. They were the ones who knew her best in the 1960s and '70s. Regarding the boomer audiences King said, "They have connected with me and, in connecting with me, they're really connecting with themselves and thinking of where they were when they first heard one of my songs."

The reason why we enjoy music so much is because of its connective quality. We connect to a message, a place, a person, or a memory. That connection continues to interpret and sustain life for us, as it gives us a sense of purpose and meaning.

The *Britannica Encyclopedia* defines music as, "art concerned with combining vocal or instrumental sounds for beauty of form or emotional expression, usually according to cultural standards of rhythm, melody, and in most Western music, harmony." The important point for us is the phrase "emotional expression." Music often articulates that which we feel but are unable to put into grammatical sentences.

Paul concluded his letter to Rome with a doxology. Doxology comes from the two Greek words *doxa* and *logos*. These two words basically mean "words of praise." Paul chose to close his letter with a doxology for the purpose of emotional expression. For Paul knew that words of praise best expressed the theological message contained in the previous pages of his letter. It is a message that we praise God for revealing to us through Jesus Christ our relationship with the God.

Doxologies are found in almost every book of the New Testament. These were doxologies that were used in worship in the first-century church. Hearing the doxology read in a letter, congregations would understand why the author of the letter wanted to give glory to God. They could sing a doxology of praise when they learned of the letter's message of forgiveness, of the message of salvation, and of the message of a personal God. It is for these reasons that we today sing doxologies in worship.

The use of hymns and doxologies for emotional expression was always a part of the liturgy of the early church. The Fourth Ecumenical Council, also known as the Council of Chalcedon, was a church council held from October to November in the year

451 AD. Chalcedon was an ancient maritime town in a region of the Roman Empire in northwest Asia Minor. At this council we were afforded the Latin hymn of praise called *Te Deum*, with the English translation being "A Song of the Church." The hymn begins with this stanza:

> *Thou art the King of Glory, O Christ,*
> *Thou art the everlasting Son of the Father*

"A Song of the Church" is a hymn of praise and adoration. It is a hymn that expresses our devotion and submission to God. "A Song of the Church" is most certainly a hymn we could sing in our worship service today.

Tomorrow we will be celebrating Christmas Day. The doxology *Gloria in excelsis* becomes important for us. This was the doxology sung by the angels when they announced the birth of Jesus to the shepherds. The words come to us from Luke's gospel and are probably familiar to all of us. The angels sang:

> *"Glory to God in the highest heaven,*
> *and on earth peace to those on whom his favor rests."*

The doxology *Gloria in excelsis* is often called the "Angel's Hymn." It is regarded by the church as the Greater Doxology. By the year 500 it was sung in churches before the scripture reading. The Greater Doxology was used with the same purpose that Paul used his doxology at the conclusion of his letter to the church in Rome. It was used for emotional expression.

What emotion did Paul want to express? Paul was singing a doxology because God had, in Paul's words, "revealed the mystery that was kept a secret for ages." The mystery revealed was that we now fully understood the gospel message. It was a mystery that the Old Testament prophets understood vaguely, but we now understand fully. It was a mystery that has been revealed through Jesus Christ. We now know, through Jesus Christ, the eternal plan of God.

And what is the eternal plan of God that was revealed in Jesus Christ? It is all the theological doctrines that Paul presented in his letter to the church in Rome. The first half of the word theology is *theo* that means *God* in Greek. The suffix *-logy* means "the study of." So, theology literally means "the study of god." The letter that Paul wrote to the church in Rome was his most theological dissertation. In this letter, more than any other, Paul systematically outlined what he believed.

The theology that Paul presented in Romans was that the gospel was the power of God for salvation for both Jews and Gentiles. Paul believed that sin was a universal human condition and that people could only be saved by grace. Paul exhorted Christians to present their bodies as living sacrifices, remaining obedient to the teachings of Jesus. For this message Paul sang a doxology, a hymn of praise.

Today is the fourth and last Sunday of Advent. The word Advent comes from the Latin word *adventus*, which means "coming" or "arrival." The Advent season is focused on the coming of Jesus as the Messiah.

Most churches have an Advent wreath with five candles. The four outer candles are lit during the four Sundays of Advent, and the center candle is lit on Christmas Day. Various meanings have been associated with each candle, but the interpretation that I now present is appropriate as it corresponds with Paul's message in his letter to the church in Rome.

The first candle represents Isaiah who prophesied of the coming of the Messiah. The second candle represents the Bible, the Word of God. The third candle represents Mary, the mother of Jesus. The fourth candle represents John the Baptist, Jesus' cousin, who told the people in Israel to get ready for the coming of the Messiah. The middle candle is lit on Christmas Day and represents the Messiah, Jesus, the light of the world. Three of the candles are purple. On the third Sunday, which represents Mary, the color is pink. The center candle is always white as it represents Christ.

Purple is the liturgical color for Advent. Purple symbolizes the sovereignty of Christ who is the Messiah. Purple is the color of royalty as we celebrate the coming of the King of kings. Purple is an appropriate symbolic color to represent the message of Advent, for Advent is the season of the Christian year in which we prepare ourselves for the coming Messiah.

Purple is also the color used in Lent for it symbolizes penitence, which is the message of Lent. The selection of the color purple for both the liturgical season of Advent and the liturgical season of Lent is not arbitrary. The color purple that is used in Advent and Lent shows the connection between Jesus' birth and death. The Incarnation cannot be separated from the crucifixion.

Our lectionary reading for this worship service is appropriate for it represents Paul's understanding of Advent, as well as the church's understanding of Advent through the centuries. It is the message that during the last four sabbaths we have prepared ourselves for the mystery that will be revealed tomorrow on Christmas Day. It is the message that the Messiah has come and the world has been redeemed.

Tomorrow is Christmas Day. Do you feel spiritually prepared? Do you feel you can approach the manger with the same sacredness as the shepherds? Do you feel you can show the same adoration as the three wise men? Do you feel like you are ready to sing a doxology of praise?

Tonight there will be many festivities — which is good. We should have a time of merriment. But, there should be a pause in the merriment to reflect on what we shall be celebrating tomorrow morning. We should be sure that we have prepared ourselves to come to worship on Christmas Day with contrite and penitent hearts.

Johann Sebastian Bach, who was born in Germany in 1685, was a great composer and church organist. He considered church music to be sacred. Bach once said, "I play the notes as they are written but it is God who makes the music."

Bach's love for music can be understood from this story from his childhood. Johann's parents died when he was a young boy, so he lived with his brother, who was a church organist. Johann wanted to learn and play music, but his brother kept his music locked away, since he thought it is too valuable to be used by children. So each night, when everyone was asleep, Johann, with candle in hand, quietly crept down the stairs to the study. He carefully opened the door to the study so it would not squeak. He then went over to the locked cabinet and squeezed his arm through the lattice. He carefully grabbed a manuscript and spread the precious pages out on the table. The rest of his night was spent carefully copying the notes of the music. He would then begin to learn this piece in the morning.

When Johann was an adult and an established church organist and composer, he still believed music to be sacred. Realizing his compositions were inspired by God he always followed this sacred ritual. Whenever he began a new piece of music, he bowed his head and prayed. Without Jesus' help, Bach knew he'd never be able to complete the task of composing. Before writing even one note, Bach carefully formed the letters J J at the top of the page. The letters stood for *Jesu Juva*, which means "Jesus, Help!" Bach knew he could best compose a piece of music with the help of Jesus.

When Bach completed his composition, he wrote the letters SDG at the bottom of the last page of his composition. The letters SDG stood for "Soli Deo Gloria," which means "For the Glory of God Alone." Bach hoped that when the music was played, it would point toward the glory of God.

On this last Sunday of Advent as we prepare our hearts and souls for Christmas morning, let us join together in singing the "Angel's Hymn":

*"Glory to God in the highest heaven,
and on earth peace to those on whom his favor rests."*

Amen.

Christmas Eve / Day
Titus 2:11-14

In diem natalem

For the grace of God has appeared, bringing salvation to all, training us to renounce impiety and worldly passions, and in the present age to live lives that are self-controlled, upright, and godly, while we wait for the blessed hope and the manifestation of the glory of our great God and Savior, Jesus Christ. He it is who gave himself for us that he might redeem us from all iniquity and purify for himself a people of his own who are zealous for good deeds.
Titus 2:11-14

John Wesley was the founding father of the Methodist denomination. Even though he had been leading his followers throughout England for several years preaching repentance, Wesley himself still questioned the validity of his own faith. While leading and inspiring others, Wesley's was consumed with doubts regarding his own salvation.

Wesley felt depressed and dejected for his seeming lack of faith. Realizing this, a few friends compelled Wesley to accompany them to a Moravian society meeting in a room on Aldersgate Street, a few blocks away from St. Paul's Cathedral in London. Wesley unwillingly attended the prayer meeting, but in doing so his life was transformed. While attending that Moravian prayer meeting, Wesley heard a reading from the book of Romans. That passage that he heard is still unknown to us today, but it transformed Wesley and gave him the assurance of his salvation.

Regarding that experience, Wesley wrote in his Journal on May 24, 1738, "In the evening I went very unwillingly to a society in Aldersgate Street, where one was reading Luther's preface to the epistle to the Romans. About a quarter before nine, while the leader was describing the change which God works in the heart through faith in Christ, I felt my heart strangely warmed. I felt I did trust in Christ alone for salvation; and an assurance was given me that he had taken away my sins, even mine, and saved me from the law of sin and death."

"I felt my heart strangely warmed." This has become one of the catch phrases that has defined Methodism. It is used today exactly in the same way that John Wesley intended it when he wrote it in his journal. "I felt my heart strangely warmed." I am assured of my salvation. I no longer harbor any doubts. I am no longer uncertain. I know I have been saved by grace through the Lord Jesus Christ.

This is the message of Christmas that we celebrate this morning. With the coming of the Christ child we have been saved from our sins. We are forgiven. We know with assurance that heaven will be our final resting place.

In Latin Christmas means "Christ mass." Christmas is a mass, it is a worship service where we celebrate Christ's birth on Christmas Day. The celebration of Christmas was not an important event for the first four centuries of the early church. It was during these centuries that the church focused on the death and resurrection of Jesus. This made Good Friday and Easter Sunday the most important events for the church during the liturgical year.

Christmas was recognized during these centuries, but to a much lesser degree. There was no common understanding among the various churches on how and when to celebrate the birth of Christ. Therefore, the Christmas Day celebration took place on various dates throughout Christendom. How these dates were selected varied from church to church.

Some used the vernal equinox. The vernal equinox is the time at which the sun crosses the plane of the equator toward the relevant hemisphere, making night and day of equal length. It occurs about March 21 in the Northern hemisphere.

Another date for the birth of Jesus was on the fourth day of creation. This is the day God created the sun and since Jesus is the "sun of righteousness" he was also born on this day of light.

Another popular date for the birth of Jesus was January 6, which is Epiphany. This is the day on which we celebrate the baptism of Jesus. Those who promoted this date considered Jesus just to be human at his birth. He was not divine until the Holy Spirit in the form of a dove descended upon him during his baptism. It was then that Jesus as a human being was incarnate with the Spirit of God.

This was the most popular view that was circulating around the early church. It was also the most heretical doctrine because it denied the incarnation of Jesus at conception, and caused the church fathers to realize that a date for the birth of Jesus had to be officially established.

The date selected was December 25. One reason for its selection is that it came before January 6, which is the date for the celebration of the Baptism of Our Lord in the liturgical season of Epiphany. With the church officially recognizing the birth and incarnation of Jesus on December 25, the date of January 6 could no longer be defended.

Another reason for this date, and the reason you may be most familiar with, is on December 25 there was a great secular celebration in honor of *Sol Invictus*, who was worshiped as "The Invincible Sun." *Sol Invictus* was the sun God of the Romans. The celebration of *Sol Invictus* went far beyond mere merriment to actually debauchery. The lack of social restraints that allowed someone to indulge in all sorts of mischievous behavior attracted some Christians to the festivities. The attractiveness of the celebration's activities certainly made it easy for the flesh to rule over the spirit.

The church leaders knew they needed to draw Christians away from this secular pagan holiday, and determined that celebrating Christmas was one of the best ways to do it. The selection of December 25 not only countered the heresy of the January 6 celebration of the baptism of Jesus, it also denounced the celebration of *Sol Invictus*. The selection of December 25 also cleared up another dispute in the church; now all congregations would celebrate the birth of Jesus on the same day.

John Chrysostom was an early church father and was the Archbishop of Constantinople. He was known for his ability to preach and for his skill at public speaking.

Chrysostom delivered his well-known Christmas sermon *In diem natalem*. The title of this sermon in Latin means the following: *In diem* means "in the day of," and *natalem* means "birth." So, the title of Chrysostom's Christmas sermon *In diem natalem* means "In the Day of the Birth." What is interesting is that *natalem* can actually mean "birthday."

Chrysostom preached this sermon in Antioch in the year 386. By this year at the end of the fourth century, it had become universally accepted that the celebration of Christmas would be on December 25.

In his sermon Chrysostom expressed the joy we all feel on Christmas morning. Chrysostom preached, "God was seen on earth through flesh and dwelt among humankind. So then, beloved, let us rejoice with great gladness. For if John leapt in his mother's womb when Mary visited Elizabeth, consider that we have actually seen our Savior born today. So now we, much more, must leap, rejoice, and be full of wonder and astonishment at the grandeur of God's plan which exceeds all thought. Think how great it would be to see the sun coming down from the heavens, running on the earth and sending out its beams on everybody from here."

This is the same joyous celebration we experience today. From Chrysostom's sermon we learn that in Jesus we see God on earth in the flesh. As John leapt in the womb of Elizabeth, we who have seen Jesus also leap and rejoice. On Christmas Day we know that God has come down from the heavens to earth, and we are bathed in the beams of God's light.

Christmas did not really become secularized until the middle of the nineteenth century. In the mid-nineteenth century Christmas began to acquire its association with an increasing secularized holiday of gift-giving and good cheer. This view was popularized in Clarke Moore's poem *A Visit from St. Nicholas* in 1823, and Charles Dicken's story *A Christmas Carol* in 1843. These are stories that we love to hear during Christmas, but their emphasis on Jesus was shadowed as benevolence became the theme. Christmas cards first appeared in 1846, and from there one secular tradition after another was added.

It is not wrong to participate in these secular traditions, if they don't take precedence over the study of the birth story in Luke's gospel and celebrating "Christ Mass."

Chrysostom preached in his sermon *In diem natalem* these sobering words, "He will reward you for this enthusiasm. Your heartfelt zeal for this day is a great sign of your love for the one who is born." The birth of Jesus should make us enthusiastic to serve him. We should have a heartfelt zeal in sharing the Christmas love we have experienced this day with others.

New Testament scholar William Barclay wrote in his commentary on Titus that our scripture reading for this morning, this Christmas morning, that "There are few passages in the New Testament that so vividly set out the moral power of the incarnation as this does." William Barclay, who published a commentary series on the New Testament in 1955 and which is still read today, was a professor of Biblical Criticism at the University of Glasgow. Barclay is an exegetical scholar who must be taken very seriously for his knowledge and insight into the scriptures.

He stressed the moral power of the incarnation. The incarnation is the embodiment of God's spirit in Jesus, allowing us to confess on Christmas Day that Jesus was fully God, fully man. This is the moral power of the incarnation that is proclaimed on Christmas Day. This is the moral power that is seen throughout the ministry of Jesus that changes lives.

Those who knelt before the manger in Bethlehem were never the same again. John Wesley while attending a societal meeting in a room at Aldersgate Street had his own form of a manger, and he was never the same again. Where is the manger that changed your life? Where did the Christmas experience happen for you? When did you come to be able to say, "I felt my heart strangely warmed."

Did your Christmas experience, whether it happened on December 25 or another day of the year, make you enthusiastic to serve Jesus? Did your Christmas experience give you a heartfelt zeal to share the love of Jesus? Did the moral power of the incarnate Christ bring you salvation and a transformed life?

In our lectionary reading, Paul began his discussion of the meaning of the birth of Christ with these words, "bringing salvation to all." For Paul, the Christmas story is a story of salvation. It is the story that we will have an Aldersgate experience. The moral power of the incarnation will have us accept Jesus Christ as our

Lord and Savior, and by grace we will experience salvation. We will know what it means to be forgiven.

But Paul then wrote if the Christmas story brings us to accept Jesus as our Savior then we must live, in Paul's words, "to renounce impiety and worldly passions, and in the present age to live lives that are self-controlled, upright, and godly." The moral power that brings us to salvation is the same moral power that changes how we live.

We no longer attend the festivities of *Sol Invictus*, who was the Roman god worshiped as "The Invincible Sun." We have surrendered that debauchery way of life. We now desire to live a life that is "self-controlled, upright, and godly."

To live a life, in Paul's words, that is self-controlled, upright, and godly, is not an easy mandate. It does require self-discipline. It does require us to be engaged daily in private spiritual meditation. It does require us to be a part of a worshiping congregation that celebrates Christ-mass each sabbath. But Paul expects those who are saved to live a life that demonstrates that salvation. Once you feel your heart strangely warmed, it becomes imperative that you are engaged in activities that will continue to warm your heart.

Apollo 8 was the first manned space craft to enter the moon's orbit. What heightened the excitement of this historic occasion is that the spacecraft began its flight around the moon on Christmas Eve, 1968. To commemorate this special occasion and to recognize the religious significance of the date, all three astronauts — Frank Borman, James Lovell, William Andrews — decided to read passages of scripture to all the inhabitants of planet earth. The three men decided the most appropriate text would be the creation story recorded in Genesis. The Gideons presented the space voyagers with a Bible from which to do their reading. Unfortunately, the Gideon Bible was not made of fire resistant material, and the astronauts could not take it along. How, they wondered, could they carry the Genesis text into space? The solution: print the Bible passage on the flame-resistant flight plan. Therefore, each time the astronauts read the day's agenda, their eyes also fell upon the word of God. Because of this arrangement, the word of God was constantly kept before the astronauts during their entire journey in outer space.

In the foreboding darkness of space looking down upon a light blue colored planet surrounded by a white halo of clouds, and beyond that the brilliance of other planets, stars and moons, the astronauts must have truly understood the words of Isaiah, "The people walking in darkness have seen a great light." Whatever darkness one may encounter, it shall always be penetrated by the light of Christ.

As we celebrate Christmas today we do so knowing that today and every day, that every time we look at our daily agenda, we will know that we no longer walk in darkness but have seen a great light.

Amen.

Christmas 1
Galatians 4:4-7

Abba! Father!

But when the fullness of time had come, God sent his Son, born of a woman, born under the law, in order to redeem those who were under the law, so that we might receive adoption as children. And because you are children, God has sent the Spirit of his Son into our hearts, crying, "Abba! Father!" So you are no longer a slave but a child, and if a child then also an heir, through God.
Galatians 4:4-7

Joseph Mohr, a 24-year-old Austrian priest, believed he needed to instill peace and hope into the lives of his troubled and bewildered parishioners. The year was 1816, just a year after the army of Napoleon destroyed their city and countryside. The salt trade, on whose livelihood the town survived, was savagely disrupted from the fighting. The salt trade was so important to the economy that the regions capital was named Salzburg, which means "Salt City."

Mohr was an accomplished musician and he penned a poem of hope for Christmas Day, which was titled *Silent Night, Holy Night*. Two years later Mohr asked his friend, organist and teacher Franz Xaver Gruber, to set the poem to music. As mice had eaten through the bellows of the church organ, the two sang a duet accompanied by guitar.

It was during the Civil War that John Freeman Young, a priest serving Trinity Episcopal Church on Wall Street in New York City, wrote the English translation for the hymn. Young took the liberty to rearrange the verses. It is the Young arrangement that is commonly accepted throughout the world today, having been translated into 300 languages. Sadly, Young omitted Mohr's fourth verse, the one written especially to offer hope for the depressed people of Austria.

As it was originally sung in Mohr's Saint Nicholas Church in Austria, the meaning of compassion flowed forth from the candle lit sanctuary as the fourth verse was solemnly sung: "Where on this day, all power of fatherly love poured forth, and Jesus like a brother lovingly embraced the peoples of this world...."

This is Paul's message for us this first Sunday after Christmas. Jesus' loving embrace of the world has conquered the evil that surrounds us. We no longer need to be disheartened.

When Paul wrote in our lectionary reading for this morning that Jesus was "born of a woman," he was making reference to the Old Testament passage in Genesis that the "seed" of a woman will crush the head of the serpent. The passage reads, "And I will put enmity between you and the woman, and between your seed and hers; he will crush your head."

Jesus, according to Paul, came to destroy Satan. Satan can appear in our lives in many forms and with even more temptations. Perhaps we can best understand the litany of temptations and misbehaviors that Satan entices us to by listing Paul's desires of the flesh as recorded in Galatians: "The acts of the flesh are obvious: sexual immorality, impurity and debauchery, idolatry and witchcraft, hatred, discord, jealousy, fits of rage, selfish ambition, dissensions, factions and envy, drunkenness, orgies, and the like."

In this list, we can all find ourselves, and probably not just in one place but in several. If you do not think you are a card-carrying member of this list, then you can place yourself in the category of sin called self-righteousness.

We are sinners. I am afraid that we too often just play lip service to this by saying, "I am a sinner," while still believing that we are a good and decent person. But, in actuality we are all sinners. The only perfect person was Jesus. The only person absent of sin was Jesus.

We certainly are not all serial killers or rapists, but that does not excuse our many trespasses. If we go back to Paul's list of what it means to live by the flesh, to live in sin, to live under the influence of Satan, then we will take the words "I am a sinner" a little more seriously. Idolatry — what do we find in our lives that is taking precedence over Jesus? Impurity — what actions and words corrodes our souls? Jealousy — what causes us to have dissatisfaction and envy? Selfish ambition — who do we discredit for our own advancement? Nobody sitting in the pews this morning, if you are very honest with yourself, can deny that idolatry, envy, jealousy, gossip, anger, and hatred have crept into your lives. This is the power of Satan within us. We cannot deny it, but we can control it.

Jesus came from the seed of a woman to conquer and destroy Satan, to crush the head of Satan, destroying any power and control Satan can have over our lives. But, we often forget that Satan will not be completely destroyed until the coming of the Lord on judgment day. Satan will not be completely destroyed until the second coming of our Lord.

This means that during our present age we are in a spiritual warfare with Satan. We know victory is ours and Satan will be destroyed on judgment day, but until then we must battle Satan's evil influence. And we sometimes forget, or rather deny, that since it is a spiritual battle sometimes Satan wins. This is why with a loving God there can continue to be pain and suffering in the world.

Most people consider the Normandy invasion, better known as D-Day, on June 6, 1944, as the turning point of the Second World War. It was with that invasion everyone knew Nazi Germany was destroyed; but, no one knew how long it would take for Germany's ultimate destruction. We consider D-Day to be the turning point of World War II because we look at the war from a Western perspective.

But the final judgment of Germany came at the Battle of Stalingrad in Russia, which lasted from August 1942 to February 1943. After this harsh winter battle the defeated Nazis had lost the war. The invasion of France in June 1944 only hastened the destruction of the evil satanic empire of the Third Reich.

With Jesus coming from the seed of a woman we have our Battle of Stalingrad, the defeat of Satan. It is only a matter of time. You and I can hasten that day of defeat if we join the troops on the Normandy beaches.

Jesus came to crush the head of Satan, and in doing so Jesus came to redeem us from our sins. Jesus came so if we confess our sins and accept Jesus Christ as our Lord and Savior our sins will be forgiven. As Paul wrote in Galatians, which is a part of the scripture reading for this morning, Jesus came "to redeem us." Jesus is our salvation. Jesus forgives us of our sins. Jesus makes it possible for us to have a new life.

We must remember that even though we have experienced salvation, we are still soldiers in the spiritual war against Satan. It does mean that even though we have been redeemed, we will still suffer the wounds caused by our idolatry, envy, and jealousy. But, we also know that if we are sincere in our obedience to Jesus on the final judgment day we will find our names in the Book of Life. We will be able to say with Paul, as he recorded in 2 Timothy, "I have fought the good fight, I have finished the race, I have kept the faith."

Adoniram Judson was a Deist while attending Providence College, which is now Brown University. After graduation, he realized that Deism was an aimless religious belief and he converted to Christianity. Deism denies God's revelations and maintains that God does not intervene in the lives of individuals. Judson realized that this was not true for one who believes in the Christmas message of the incarnation. The Christmas message is that God does intervene, through Jesus Christ, in the world and in the lives of individuals.

Judson took upon himself the role of evangelist, and became one of the founders of the American Baptist Missionary Society. Unable to be accepted in the southeast countries of his choice, in 1812 Judson took his missionary zeal to Burma. Judson and his wife Ann were the only Christians in the entire country. After six long and exhausting years he had his first convert, Moung Nau. Undaunted, Judson continued to labor for the Lord, and by 1850 there were 210,000 Christians in Burma, which was one out of every 58 Burmans. Yet, at this time the 62-year-old evangelist began to suffer from depression and doubted his own salvation. Adoniram Judson died on a voyage back to America in an attempt to regain the assurance of his salvation.

In this spiritual battle, we will at times question if we really are saved. We will always be plagued with doubts regarding our faith. We will be plagued by those unanswerable theological questions that cause us sometimes to wonder if there really is a God. This is what makes faith so difficult and pursuing service to

God so difficult. Even Paul questioned his faith at times, but he still remained an effective evangelist. Recall what Paul wrote, "I have fought the good fight, I have finished the race, I have kept the faith."

In Paul's letter to the Christian congregations in Galatia he assured them that Christ is doing battle against Satan; but, we can also be assured by the end time that Christ will have crushed and destroyed Satan.

Our salvation protects us and liberates us from the demonic powers that roam the earth and infect our lives. Though we still experience temptation and though we still experience the pain that is caused by demons, we know we are free. We know we are saved.

We have the assurance of our salvation because we know, in Paul's words, from our lesson this morning, we are "children of God." Through Jesus Christ we have an intimate relationship with God. As Jesus, the Son of God, was able to say "Abba! Father!" now we as the children of God, the sons and daughters of God, can also say "Abba! Father!" Paul instructed us that this is possible when he wrote in our reading for this morning, "God has sent the Spirit of his Son into our hearts, crying, 'Abba! Father!'"

Abba! Father! is Aramaic. It was the language spoken by Jesus. When the New Testament gospels and letters were written the words "Abba! Father!" were not translated into Greek, but they were written in the original Aramaic. These words by Jesus had such a powerful meaning for the early church that the writers felt compelled to keep the original Aramaic language as it was spoken by Jesus. It is not a trivialization to say that "Abba! Father!" means "daddy." Daddy and Mommy are probably the two most intimate words we can utter.

Jesus and his disciples read Hebrew in the synagogue, but in everyday speech and preaching they used a closely related language to Hebrew which was Aramaic. In Aramaic *abba* is a word derived from baby-language. The Jewish rabbis taught that a small child learns to say *abba,* which means "daddy" and *imma,* which means "mommy." According to the rabbis it was proper in Judaism for an adult to continue to address one's parents using *abba* and *imma.*

In the Garden of Gethsemane, when he was confronted with his death by crucifixion, Jesus began his prayer by saying "Daddy." Jesus prayed, "'Abba, Father,' everything is possible for you. Take this cup from me. Yet not what I will, but what you will."

This personal relationship that Jesus had with God is ours as well. This is one of the real joys that we celebrate during the Christmas season. It is the feeling of intimacy when we can call God "daddy."

Maybe one of the best ways to understand what it means for us to be able to call our heavenly Father daddy is to recall a teaching by Jesus. Remember the lesson of Jesus, as recorded in Luke's gospel, of the parent child relationship we have with God. Jesus said, "Which of you fathers, if your son asks for a fish, will give him a snake instead? Or if he asks for an egg, will give him a scorpion? If you then, though you are evil, know how to give good gifts to your children, how much more will your Father in heaven give the Holy Spirit to those who ask him!"

All of the mothers and fathers seated in the sanctuary are evil only in the sense that we are imperfect sinners. We are not evil in the sense in that we deliberately abuse our children. Despite our faults as individuals, as parents the care, love, and devotion we have for our children cannot be measured.

We are happy when our children are happy. We are sad when our children are sad. When our children are sick, we feel their pain. When our children are disappointed, we do what we can to give them hope. And there are those times when an illness or a sorrow overcomes our child, and we have that terrible, awful feeling of helplessness that we cannot make things better.

God's love for us is far greater than any love we can express as a parent to our child.

Country western singers, Tim McGraw and Faith Hill, were married in 1996. They have three daughters, Gracie, Maggie, and Audrey. The couple has a family rule that they will never spend more than three consecutive days apart from their three children. Tim McGraw expressed what it is like being a parent with these words, "We're parents first, and once you have kids, everybody knows that you have priority lists. Number one is your family and everything else just kind of finds its place."

On this first Sunday after Christmas Day, it is reassuring to know that when our heavenly parent looked down into the manger, perhaps he saw your face and my face as well.

Amen.

Epiphany of the Lord
Ephesians 3:1-12

The Foot-board of the Pulpit and the Floor of the Parlor

This is the reason that I Paul am a prisoner for Christ Jesus for the sake of you Gentiles — for surely you have already heard of the commission of God's grace that was given me for you, and how the mystery was made known to me by revelation, as I wrote above in a few words, a reading of which will enable you to perceive my understanding of the mystery of Christ. In former generations this mystery was not made known to humankind, as it has now been revealed to his holy apostles and prophets by the Spirit: that is, the Gentiles have become fellow heirs, members of the same body, and sharers in the promise in Christ Jesus through the gospel. Of this gospel I have become a servant according to the gift of God's grace that was given me by the working of his power. Although I am the very least of all the saints, this grace was given to me to bring to the Gentiles the news of the boundless riches of Christ, and to make everyone see what is the plan of the mystery hidden for ages in God who created all things; so that through the church the wisdom of God in its rich variety might now be made known to the rulers and authorities in the heavenly places. This was in accordance with the eternal purpose that he has carried out in Christ Jesus our Lord, in whom we have access to God in boldness and confidence through faith in him.
Ephesians 3:1-12

Aldhelm, at the age of 65, was appointed as the bishop of Sherborne, in England. Aldhelm lived from the year 640 to the year 709. As an English scholar, Aldhelm studied Roman law, astronomy, astrology, Hebrew, and Greek. His fame as a scholar rapidly spread into other countries across Europe.

After Aldhelm was appointment as bishop, he spent the next four years walking from one end of his parish to the other preaching in every village and town until his death on May 25, 709, at the age of 69. Aldhelm died while on one of his preaching tours.

Aldhelm was a gifted musician and poet. He would set his own compositions to music, but none of his songs, which were popular during his lifetime, have been preserved for us today.

Aldhelm's realized that his people were slow to come to church. To encourage them to attend worship, Aldhelm would preach in public places, in the markets, and at the foot of bridges singing songs in the vernacular of the people. When a crowd would gather, he would introduce the religious themes into his songs. It was his desire to awaken the interest of those gathered in the gospel message.

Aldhelm wrote in elaborate and eloquent Latin. Aldhelm was much admired by those in academia, but his fame as a scholar declined among the English nobility and clergy. But, Aldhelm's reputation as a pioneer in Latin scholarship in England remains to this day.

As we can see from the life of Aldhelm, that preaching is not confined to the pulpit. We can preach the gospel message wherever we are, which could be in public places, the market, or even at the foot of a bridge.

More realistic for you who are gathered in the sanctuary this morning, and do not find the pulpit to be your home for preaching, you do have many other pulpits from which to preach in the course of the day. The pulpits from which you preach will not be a high overpowering ornate carved wooden structure where I am standing at this very moment; but, the place from which you stand as you proclaim the gospel message will have the same symbolic significance as a sanctuary pulpit.

When we discuss preaching in the public square the same questions always arise. I have no place to preach. I have no one to preach to. I do not know what to say. I have other spiritual gifts, and preaching is not one of them. I lack the confidence to preach. I am too shy to preach. I would look like a fool. With that litany of excuses, we have successfully excluded ourselves from the ministry of evangelism.

William Booth, who lived from 1829 to 1912, was the founder of the Salvation Army in England. He was known for his strong evangelical preaching for which he was never ashamed. He was also known to preach at every opportunity that was afforded him.

Once, Booth was literally standing on a soap box at an intersection in London. He was expounding the gospel in a loud voice and with great enthusiasm. He was also preaching a very strong and uncompromising message for the need of sinners to repent. A lady standing in the crowd shouted a complaint at Booth, chastising him for his public display that she considered bombastic and inappropriate for a preacher to be standing on a soap box in downtown London. Unfazed by this criticism and condemnation, Booth quickly retorted to the woman, "I like my way of doing it more than your way of not doing it."

"I like my way of doing it more than your way of not doing it." Those are the words that ought to motivate us whenever we think we have no venue or no place to preach. We must ask, "Where is my soap box on a London street corner?" It takes only a little imagination to find our London street corner. What does take great imagination is courage and confidence to get up on that soap box.

If we should decide that, "I like my way of doing it more than your way of not doing it," then we will find opportunities to share the gospel message. We will probably never do it as a great oration from street corner soap box; but, in casual conversation we will be standing at the crosswalk with the opportunity to make a difference in the life of another individual.

Our places of employment do prevent us from being bombastic outspoken evangelists. But, there will be a time when talking to a colleague and sharing the gospel message would be appropriate and willingly listened to. The same would be true for our neighbors, and those with whom we socialize with at clubs and other activities.

Ralph Waldo Emerson was known as an essayist, lecturer, and poet. Emerson, during his lifetime, was professionally addressed as Waldo Emerson. He delivered more than 1,500 public lectures across the United States. Emerson was ordained a congregation minister, and for several years pastored Second Church in Boston.

Regarding preaching, Emerson realized that the person in the pulpit must witness in language that is easily understood and relevant to his audience. In a lecture titled, *The Preacher*, delivered in May 1879 at the Divinity Hall Chapel in Cambridge, Emerson said, "And if I had to counsel a young preacher, I should say, 'When there is any difference felt between the foot-board of the pulpit and the floor of the parlor, you have not yet said that which you should say.'"

Our sharing the word of God should be directed to individuals in their daily encounter with the adversities of life. Our counsel from the scriptures ought to be simple and practical, yet pertinent enough to offer assurances in the promises of Jesus. In this endeavor, we cannot cease from our labors.

The words, "When there is any difference felt between the foot-board of the pulpit and the floor of the parlor, you have not yet said that which you should say," must be our guide in sharing the gospel message. We share a message that is relevant to where the people are who standing before us. Our message is not esoteric. Our message is not obtuse. Our message is not enigmatic. But, our message is pragmatic. Our message is applicable. Our message is pertinent.

We do not need to be biblical scholars or systematic theologians to share this message. We do not need to know the meaning of every Bible verse. We do not need to have a theological answer for every baffling question people have regarding religion. What we do need is a sincere faith that can express what Jesus means to us personally. If we share the gospel with heartfelt sincerity, then the individual to whom we speak will be able to accept our lack of biblical knowledge.

The apostle Paul began our lectionary reading for this morning by saying he was called to preach the gospel message. Paul wrote, "Of this gospel I have become a servant…to bring the news of the boundless riches of Christ." Paul understood that his role was to preach the gospel. He implied in our lectionary reading that his calling to preach came on his Damascus Road experience, when he heard the voice of Christ calling him into ministry.

But, Paul wrote in our lectionary reading that he is not alone in that calling, but the church is also a part of the call to preach.

Paul wrote, "so that through the church the wisdom of God in its rich variety might be made known to the rulers and authorities in the heavenly places." The church, which would be you and me, is to preach the gospel message.

Paul's message is very simple and easily reflects the dictate, "When there is any difference felt between the foot-board of the pulpit and the floor of the parlor, you have not yet said that which you should say." For Paul, the foot-board of the pulpit and the floor of the parlor are connected with the message of grace.

Paul wrote of the message that was entrusted to him, and then to the church, with these words, "For surely you have already heard of the commission of God's grace that was given me for you." According to Paul, God has commissioned all of us to share the message of grace.

Paul uses the Greek word *polupoikilos* to describe the grace of God. The word *polupoikilos* means "many-colored." The implication for Paul is that the grace of God will be sufficient to sustain us during any situation in life. It means that no darkness can befall us that the light of God is unable to shine through.

Grace ought to be a message that we are all comfortable in sharing. The message of grace does not require us to be biblical scholars or professors of systematic theology. It only requires us to be sincere, honest, and heartfelt when we share how God has transformed our lives. It only requires us to be sincere, honest, and heartfelt when we share how God can change the life of the individual to whom we are witnessing.

Grace is the sincere message that we can share on how God can forgive us of our sins. Grace is the message on how God can comfort us in a time of trial and tribulation. Grace is the message that we are accepted and protected by God.

We ought to seek every opportunity to share the message of grace in the name of Jesus, with the hope of transforming the world.

United Methodist Bishop William R. Cannon was invited to give a prayer during the inauguration ceremony for president-elect Jimmy Carter. At the conclusion of his prayer, which was being nationally televised, Cannon closed his prayer by offering the prayer in the name of Jesus Christ. This action by the bishop outraged and offended people throughout the country, because he had used a religious intonation at a state event. During a press conference, the bishop endured a rash of criticisms for the public expression of his faith. Against all these derogatory remarks, the bishop defended himself by speaking one short sentence, "Jesus may not be the Savior of all the people of the United States, but he wants to be!"

Paul, in our lectionary reading, said that Jesus came for both the Jews and the Gentiles. Paul wrote, "that is, the Gentiles have become fellow heirs." By saying that the Gentiles have become fellow heirs, Paul is saying that Jesus came not only for the Jews, but for all the people for the world, that is, the Gentiles as well. As Paul noted earlier in his letter, the one unifying Christian message for everyone across the globe is the message of grace.

Our calling is to share the gospel message of grace to anyone and everyone. We share the message to friend and foe alike. We share the message to individuals of any socio-economic class. We share the message to anyone regardless of sex, age, race, and any other cultural category we might assign an individual to that would otherwise separate us.

Norman Vincent Peale was the pastor of Marble Collegiate Church in New York City for 52 years. It is the church that our current president, Donald Trump, attended when he lived in New York. Peale is probably better known for his book *The Power of Positive Thinking*, which was published in 1952. The book was part theology and part psychology as it emphasized the importance of being optimistic. It was an optimism that was based on having faith in Jesus and believing in the promises of Jesus.

Substituting for a friend, Norman Vincent Peale was to preach his first sermon at a church in Walpole, Massachusetts. Unsure of himself and feeling he lacked the ability to write a sermon and then preach it, Norman sent his father, Charles Clifford Peale, who was a Methodist minister, a telegram: "Preaching next Sunday. Stop. Please send sermon. Stop."

Norman knew that his father, a physician who had become a Methodist minister, would have a dynamic sermon for his son to preach on his first Sunday in the pulpit. Charles Peale responded immediately to his son's request, replying with this telegram:

"Suggest text John 10:10. Stop. Preach your own sermon. Stop. Good luck. Stop. Dad. Stop." Realizing that he was on his own, Norman wrote a sermon to the text shared by his father: "I have come that they might have life, and that they might have it more abundantly."

On Sunday morning Norman looked out the window of the church's study, watching the people entering the sanctuary, wondering what he could say to them that would lift their spirits. One man in particular caught Norman's attention, a stately old gentleman, whose head was lowered as he walked. There was a look of sadness and trouble on that stately old gentleman's face.

Norman stepped into the pulpit and preached on the wisdom and love of Jesus, and how he can change our defeats into victories. After the service the stately old gentleman greeted the young preacher at the door, commenting, "You have read my mind. I needed help, and you gave me that help in your sermon." At that moment, Norman Vincent Peale learned the secret to successful preaching and witnessing — make it personal.

Share with others the Christ you know personally, telling them everything about the grace of Christ that you have personally experienced and have come to understand.

Amen.

Epiphany 2
1 Corinthians 6:12-20

Our Magic Mirror

"All things are lawful for me," but not all things are beneficial. "All things are lawful for me," but I will not be dominated by anything. "Food is meant for the stomach and the stomach for food," and God will destroy both one and the other. The body is meant not for fornication but for the Lord, and the Lord for the body. And God raised the Lord and will also raise us by his power. Do you not know that your bodies are members of Christ? Should I therefore take the members of Christ and make them members of a prostitute? Never! Do you not know that whoever is united to a prostitute becomes one body with her? For it is said, "The two shall be one flesh." But anyone united to the Lord becomes one spirit with him. Shun fornication! Every sin that a person commits is outside the body; but the fornicator sins against the body itself. Or do you not know that your body is a temple of the Holy Spirit within you, which you have from God, and that you are not your own? For you were bought with a price; therefore glorify God in your body.
1 Corinthians 6:12-20

Frederick Douglass approached the front door of the White House, seeking admission into Abraham Lincoln's second inaugural ball. Just as Douglass was about to knock on the door, two policemen seized him, barring the black man's entrance. Douglass, a large, powerful man, brushed the officers aside and stepped into the foyer. Once inside, two more officers, while uttering racial slurs, grabbed the uninvited guest. As Douglass was being dragged from the hall, he cried to a nearby patron, "Just say to Mr. Lincoln that Fred Douglass is at the door!" Confusion ensued.

Then suddenly the officers received orders to usher Douglass into the East Room. In that beautiful room, the great abolitionist stood in the presence of the esteemed emancipator. The place quieted as Lincoln approached his newly arrived guest, hand outstretched in greeting, and speaking in a voice loud enough so none could mistake his intent, the president announced, "Here comes my friend Douglass."

In our lectionary reading for this morning the apostle Paul instructed us that the life we live will identify us as either a Christian or a heathen. Our Christian lifestyle and our Christian identity are inseparably linked. We can stand in the East Room and remain deaf to the cries of a forsaken individual; or, we can stand in the East Room and hear the voice of a friend.

That day, during the inaugural ball, Abraham Lincoln was being judged by his peers as to the sincerity of his Christian commitment. That day, during the inaugural ball, Lincoln was being judged if what he said was also reflected in what he did. That day, during the inaugural ball, people wanted to know if Lincoln's Christian identity was connected to his Christian lifestyle.

Our place in history may not be as dramatic as the East Room of the White House; but nonetheless, people will constantly be observing us, wondering if our claim to be a Christian is genuine or a mere façade.

Paul from our lectionary reading for this morning wrote, "Do you not know that your bodies are members of Christ? Should I therefore take the members of Christ and make them members of a prostitute? Never!" Paul is asking if we are going to associate ourselves with the purity of Christ or with an individual of ill-repute.

Our reputation and our witness as a Christian are outlined in this one sentence from Paul. It is the question of how are we going to live our lives. It is a question of what will be our moral standard. It is a question of how will people observe our Christian life-style.

It is a question that concerned Jesus. It was a question that concerned Peter. It is a question that now concerns Paul. It is a question that plagued the church from the day it was conceived; and, it is a question that still resonates in the church today.

Ethnocentrism — it was the first internal conflict the Christian church experienced. Ethnocentrism considers one's own ethnic group as superior to all others; therefore, viewing alien cultures with distain. It is the audacity of superiority. It is rife with judgment. It is void of compromise. It is an intolerable self-righteousness.

Ethnocentrism is the Christian church — past, present, and future.

After a harmonious and homogenous infancy, ethnocentrism emerged during the church's adolescence. Approximately seventeen years after the crucifixion of Jesus the dispute erupted. Paul met with James, who was the brother of Jesus, in Jerusalem. Paul maintained that the grace bestowed by Jesus fulfilled the laws of Judaism, nullifying adherence. James acknowledged Jesus as the Messiah but held forth that circumcision, dietary laws, and all other Jewish mandates must still be obeyed. Unable to compromise it was agreed that Paul would be a missionary to the Gentile cities, while James remained the patriarch of the church in Jerusalem. As a sign of reconciliation Paul would send money from the affluent seacoast cities to the impoverished inner city church in Jerusalem. It was money, not a spirit of solidarity, which became the totem of unity.

It was an ethnic controversy that emerged. Paul preached that Gentiles need not become Jews and James declared that all Christians must be observant Jews. Redemption was displaced by identity. To be a Christian you must think as I think, act as I act, believe as I believe. A believer must be a member of my group, or otherwise be ostracized.

Jesus foretold this, but his message went unobserved. Jesus said, "Woe to you scribes and Pharisees, hypocrites that you are." Jesus never judged sinners, only hypocrites. Jesus acknowledged sin and cautioned against sins destructive ramifications. Yet, he offered forgiveness coupled with an admonishment to change.

Jesus only judged hypocrites, with the most visual being the Pharisees. The Pharisees demanded that individuals adhere to theological standards that they themselves avoided. Anyone who did not live as a Pharisee pretended to live was dismissed. Thus, in Jesus estimation, they were like whitewashed tombs, clean to the observer but filthy within.

Palestine was Hellenized. Hellenization is when a country accepts Greek culture to the extent that it replaces its own customs, traditions, and language. Living in Palestine, Jesus understood Greek culture and used it in his teachings.

The word hypocrisy comes from Greek theater. An actor appeared on stage as someone whom he was not off stage. The actor was a hypocrite as he appeared as two different people — one person in public but a different person in private.

The Pharisees were judged by Jesus as hypocrites for their disobedience, having expectations of others that they themselves failed to practice. The Pharisees according to Jesus were hypocrites because they appeared in public making demands on people that they themselves could not adhere to in private. As mentioned earlier, according to Jesus this made the Pharisees like white washed tombs, clean to the observer but filthy within.

A hypocrite is a Christian who thinks of himself as purer than others, when in fact he needs to be distilled.

It is hypocrites that pollute the pews of the sanctuary, keeping unbelievers away. Worshipers apologize for their incongruent behavior by saying the church is a hospital for sinners. If that were true every bed would be taken — but instead there are many empty beds because in our self-righteousness we don't feel the need for a transfusion. For us the communion rail is really a judgment seat where anyone who is different is shunned. The Pharisees wondered how could a Samaritan be good?

In the Brothers Grimm's fairy tale *Snow White*, we are like the wicked queen who constantly looks into her mirror asking, "Magic mirror on the wall, who is the fairest one of all?" The only response that the queen is interested in hearing is that she is the fairest of them all — that she is the most beautiful — that she is the most important.

We expect the same response when we look into our own magic mirrors. The message we hear is that *I cannot be accused of ethnocentrism. I cannot be called a hypocrite. I have no need for a bed in the hospital for sinners, but I will gladly connect the IV to those who are.* How truthful is our magic mirror?

It has taken centuries for us to invite African Americans down from the balcony. Women rode the wave of the feminist movement to acquire ordination. Homosexuals are slowly making their way down the center aisle. Yet, so many still wait to be beckoned from the lepers' colony, assigned there only because they are different. Are not the mentally ill still regarded as uncircumcised?

One day the wicked queen heard a different message from her magic mirror that sent her into a self-righteous rampage. The scene reads as follows:

Magic Mirror: Famed is thy beauty, Majesty. But hold, a lovely maid I see. Rags cannot hide her gentle grace. Alas, she is more fair than thee.
Queen: Alas for her! Reveal her name.
Magic Mirror: Lips red as the rose. Hair black as ebony. Skin white as snow.
Queen: Snow White!

Can we really accept Snow White into our fellowship if it forces us to see our own blemishes?

Rather than having denominations unified by Christ they are separated by polity. As Christians we look at anyone who is not like us to be a follower of a false doctrine. It is time that Christians polish those mirrors so we can see ourselves as we truly are. As James wrote, "Anyone who listens to the word but does not do what it says is like someone who looks at his face in a mirror and, after looking at himself, goes away and immediately forgets what he looks like."

We need to remember what we look like. That is the message of Paul in our lectionary lesson for this morning. What we see in the mirror everyone sees. We may think that makeup can hide our blemishes, but makeup does eventually rub off. We can only pretend for so long until people will know that who we say we are is not the same as who we really are. People will know if our Christian lifestyle and our Christian identity our inseparably linked.

The United Methodist Church has a motto that most churches and Christians would subscribe to: "Open Hearts, Open Minds, Open Doors."

Do these words describe our Christian character? Are these words the actual scenario for our churches? The real answer is more often that those who are disfigured would find a closed heart and a closed mind secured by a locked door. Standing guard is a Pharisee, arms folded and scowling, blinded by the silver crucifix dangling from his neck.

It is time that we no longer find Snow White and her Seven Dwarfs as threatening.

Paul continued his message that our Christian life-style and our Christian identity are inseparably linked when he wrote a sentence that most of us are familiar with and often quote. Paul wrote, "Or do you not know that your body is a temple of the Holy Spirit within you?"

Our body is the temple of the Holy Spirit. We have learned that our Christian lifestyle and our Christian identity our inseparably linked. We now must add that our Christian lifestyle and our Christian identity are representative of Christ dwelling within us, as we are the temple of the Holy Spirit.

We have been baptized. The Holy Spirit has descended upon us like a dove. The heavens have opened and we have heard God call our name. We have heard the voice of God say you are my child "whom I love; with whom I am well pleased."

Is God pleased with the way you live your life? Is God pleased that your lifestyle reflects your Christian identity that is wholesome and good? Is your temple clean, or does it need a good spring cleaning?

No matter how thorough we are in our cleaning, there will still be a cobweb in the corner of the ceiling and a dust ball under the cabinet — but that is far different than having carpets that have never been vacuumed and enough dust to create a gray hue on the end tables.

If we take seriously that our bodies are the temple of the Holy Spirit, then we will do what we can to be acceptable before God. In the words of Paul written in Romans, "Therefore I urge you, brethren, by the mercies of God, to present your bodies a living and holy sacrifice, acceptable to God, which is your spiritual service of worship. And do not be conformed to this world, but be transformed by the renewing of your mind, so that you may prove what the will of God is, that which is good and acceptable and perfect."

How do we clean the temple so our Christian identity will parallel our Christian lifestyle? The cleaning process means we need to be spiritually disciplined. We are to read and study the Bible. We are to attend Sunday school. We are to be present in worship. We are to participate in the mission projects sponsored by the church.

It means that we take these spiritual truths and apply them to our daily living. There is no better outline of what it means to be a temple for the Holy Spirit within us than to have our lives display the list Paul presents in Galatians, "But the fruit of the Spirit is love, joy, peace, patience, kindness, goodness, faithfulness, gentleness, self-control." If we look into our magic mirror will this be the reflection that we see?

On Memorial Day 2016, President Obama solemnly laid a wreath at the Tomb of the Unknowns at Arlington National Cemetery. This ceremony came during the revelation of how veterans were being mistreated at veterans' facilities and hospitals. There were countless reports of inadequate treatment, the need to travel long distances for treatment, and waiting lists that stretched into months. This is why in his speech he said we must support the families of the fallen and still injured, "not just with words but with our actions." The former president noted that over one million Americans had died in battle and that we have a responsibility not only to honor them, but care for their loved ones. Obama said, "The Americans who rest here, and their families — the best of us, those from whom we asked everything — ask of us today only one thing in return: that we remember them."

If our Christian identity is connected to our Christian lifestyle, then we will care for others "not just with words but with our actions."

Amen.

Epiphany 3
1 Corinthians 7:29-31

Undivided Attention

I mean, brothers and sisters, the appointed time has grown short; from now on, let even those who have wives be as though they had none, and those who mourn as though they were not mourning, and those who rejoice as though they were not rejoicing, and those who buy as though they had no possessions, and those who deal with the world as though they had no dealings with it. For the present form of this world is passing away.
1 Corinthians 7:29-31

    Johann George Rapp, with a small group of followers, relocated from Germany to Pennsylvania. They came to Pennsylvania in 1803 to avoid continued religious persecution by the Lutheran Church in Wurttemberg, Germany. It was their expectation that in Pennsylvania they would have greater latitude to express their religious beliefs.

    The settlers referred to themselves as Harmonists, and referred to their utopian community as the Harmony Society, because they believed that their communal living would create harmonious living.

    After relocating their settlement twice, the group finally established their commune along the Ohio River, just northwest of Pittsburgh. They named their 3,000-acre settlement "Oekonomie," which is today better known as Old Economy Village. It was named in German as *Oekonomie*, which means economy. This was because they believed their community would receive worldwide recognition for its religious devotion and economic prosperity.

    Rapp declared, "I am a prophet, and I am called to be one." As a prophet he established Harmony to be a utopian society whose members would prepare themselves for the second coming of Jesus. In order to be properly prepared to sustain themselves through the millennium, the Harmony Society built warehouses for food and other provisions, including gold. For this reason, the Harmonists were a very industrious community. They had massive agricultural fields, factories, and manufacturing complexes. On behalf of the community, Rapp stored more than a half a million dollars of gold in his home.

Realizing the immediacy of Christ's return, Rapp imposed celibacy on its members in 1807. By 1811 the Harmony Society recruited enough individuals to boast of having 800 members.

Rapp prophesied that Christ would return on September 15, 1829, which would be three and one half years after the Sun Woman, from chapter twelve in the book of Revelation, would have ended her reign and Christ would have begun his reign on earth. Dissension grew when Rapp's prediction went unfulfilled.

In March 1832, disillusioned at the failure of Christ to return as promised, a third of the group left. Rapp continued to lead the Harmonists until his death on August 7, 1847. His last words to his followers were, "If I did not so fully believe, that the Lord has designated me to place our society before his presence in the land of Canaan, I would consider this my last."

As the Society was unable to recruit new converts, and because of their practice of celibacy they had no children to continue the society, it was forced to sell its land and disband in 1906.

Predicting the date of the second coming of Christ has appeared often during the 2,000 years since Jesus' death.

Pope Sylvester II proclaimed that the second coming would happen on the first millennium after the death of Jesus, which would have been the year 1,000. This view had such a large following of believers across Europe that decades prior to the millennium people took out loans that could not be repaid, farmers withheld the planting of crops, industries failed to modernize. When the year 1,000 came, and went, without the appearance of Jesus, Europe collapsed economically into a great depression. It was an economic depression that was so severe that it took nearly a century for the countries of the continent to economically recover.

In our most recent history, Jerry Falwell predicted in 1999 that the second coming would come any time within the next ten years.

Falwell prophesied that it would come at the time of the second millennium, or the year 2,000. And yet, we are still waiting. Falwell is known to us as the Southern Baptist pastor, televangelist, the founder of Liberty College, and the political guru who established the Moral Majority.

If we continue our current history of understanding when the second coming will occur, we should be aware of Hal Lindsey's seminal book *The Late, Great Planet Earth* published in1970.

We should also recall the *Left Behind* series composed of sixteen novels by Tim LaHaye and Jerry Jenkins, published between 1995 and 2007. These novels are still widely read, as the books expose the suffering of those who are left behind after the rapture. If you didn't read the books, you can watch the 2014 movie starring Nicolas Cage.

Paul was in somewhat of a similar predicament, but his approach was healthier than the false prophets who followed in the proceeding centuries going by the name of Rapp, Sylvester, Falwell, Lindsey, LaHaye, and the countless others who could be added. After Paul, we saw prophets who were charlatans, who were either self-serving or misguided or both. But Paul, who was an apostle and a true prophet called by God, gave us meaningful instruction on how to prepare ourselves for the second coming of Christ.

Paul did expect Jesus to return before his death. This position influenced much of his writing, especially on social issues. Paul's advice on how we should live while we are waiting for the second coming of Jesus is outlined in our lectionary reading for this morning from First Corinthians.

Paul wrote in verse 31, "and those who deal with the world as though they had no dealings with it." In verse 35, which is not a part of lectionary reading for this morning, Paul further clarified this point when he wrote, "I am saying this for your own good, not to restrict you, but that you may live in a right way in undivided devotion to the Lord."

Paul was saying as we wait for the second coming we are to do so with our undivided attention toward the Lord. Anything that would distract us from serving the Lord should be forsaken.

This is why Paul wrote that if you were single do not get married, if marriage would keep you distracted form serving the Lord.

But get married, if after the wedding night, your attention could once again be still fully focused on serving the Lord. Marriage for Paul, in this case, would be acceptable. Paul, for himself felt celibacy was best, but Paul did not impose celibacy upon anyone else besides himself.

Paul, in our lectionary reading, extended this philosophy to all aspects of living. In our employment, in our hobbies, in our social clubs, in our recreational activities, we first and foremost must be sure that we are not distracted from serving the Lord.

This parallels a teaching of Jesus. In Luke's gospel, this incident in the life of Jesus's is reported:

> *As they were walking along the road, a man said to him, "I will follow you wherever you go."*
> *Jesus replied, "Foxes have dens and birds have nests, but the Son of Man has no place to lay his head."*
> *He said to another man, "Follow me."*
> *But he replied, "Lord, first let me go and bury my father."*
> *Jesus said to him, "Let the dead bury their own dead, but you go and proclaim the kingdom of God."*
> *Still another said, "I will follow you, Lord; but first let me go back and say goodbye to my family."*
> *Jesus replied, "No one who puts a hand to the plow and looks back is fit for service in the kingdom of God."*

The message we have from Paul is one of discipleship. While we are waiting for the second coming of Jesus, be it in the first century or the twenty-first century, if something causes us to take our hands off the plow and look back, then we have failed in giving our "undivided devotion to the Lord."

The parable of the Good Samaritan tells us how to live a life of service that is not distracted. The parable of the Good Samaritan is a lesson in "undivided devotion to the Lord."

The use of allegory was most common style of preaching in the first four centuries of the church. Allegory is when you take the characters and events in a story and use them to symbolize something else. In the parable of the Good Samaritan many of the church fathers used each character and event in the story that Jesus told to represent the ministry of Jesus himself.

The best example we have of this as it relates to the parable of the Good Samaritan is a sermon preached by Origen. Origen was born in the Egyptian city of Alexandria and lived from the year 185 to the year 254. He is considered by some the first theologian of stature in the church. He wrote a sermon on almost every verse in the entire Bible.

In understanding the parable of the Good Samaritan, we must realize that the priests and Levites worked in Jerusalem, but they lived in Jericho. We must also remember that the priest and Levite were Jews, the man along the side of the road was Jewish, and the Smartian was a racial outcast. And of course, the parable is to answer the question, "And who is my neighbor?"

Origen's exegetical interpretation of the parable of the Good Samaritan reads as follows:

> *The man who was going down is Adam. Jerusalem is paradise, Jericho is the world. The robbers are hostile powers. The priest is the law, the Levite the prophet, and the Samaritan is Christ. The wounds are disobedience. The beast is the Lord's body. The stable which accepts all who enter, is the church. The two denarii mean the Father and the Son. The manager of the stable is the head of the church, to whom care has been entrusted. The fact that the Samaritan promises he will return represents the Savior's second coming.*

Origen succinctly summarized that Christ was compassionate, as represented by the Samaritan, who took the sins of all people, represented by Adam, to the inn, which is the church, where all will be accepted and forgiven until Christ returns at his final coming. The robbers are representative of the satanic powers that are conquered by Christ. The priest and Levite are representative of the law and prophets of Judaism, which Christ has fulfilled. This parable, for Origen, chronicles the entire ministry and mission of Jesus.

The compassion of Jesus has brought into the church the discarded and disgraced souls spewed along the side of the highway of life. Molested and tormented, needing healing and nourishment, and desperate for acceptance and forgiveness, the innkeepers of Christian churches are to befriend these children of God in the name of the Good Samaritan.

The parable concluded with this powerful teaching by Jesus:

"Which of these three do you think was a neighbor to the man who fell into the hands of robbers?" The expert in the law replied, "The one who had mercy on him." Jesus told him, "Go and do likewise."

We are to go and do likewise. We are to be the innkeepers and the Samaritans who are not distracted like the priest and Levite were. We may have work to do at the temple in Jerusalem and tasks to take care of back home in Jericho, but those endeavors should never prevent us from giving our undivided attention when we see an individual who needs assistance. And remember, as Origen taught, we are to do this until the second coming of Christ.

So, the message from Paul is to be less concerned about the second coming, and be more concerned about the here and now.

There is not anytime or any place where we cannot be a disciple of Jesus. There is no occasion or circumstance where we cannot exercise our calling of discipleship. At home, at work, in the community, here in the church, we can always show love, concern, and forgiveness. Wherever we are we can always offer assistance, lend a helping hand, and be Johnny-on-the-spot. We can always live with our undivided attention on serving the Lord.

It was four o'clock in the morning on Thursday, May 1, 1873, when Susi, a faithful companion of thirty years, quietly opened the door. The room was dark. A candle was retrieved and in the flickering light a man could be seen kneeling, as if in prayer. The body stretched forward upon the bed with head cradled in hand, gently resting upon the pillow.

The magnanimous medical missionary and explorer David Livingstone was dead. A resonant mourning arose among the villagers of Tshitambo, that soon echoed throughout Western Europe and America. So beloved was Livingstone that his body was enclosed in a cylinder of bark and carried 700 miles through the jungle to the coastal shore. It was there the body was placed on a ship for the voyage to London, with an interment in Westminster Abbey. The body was reinstated in the country of his birth; but, only the body. The heart had been removed and solemnly buried in the African soil of the country to which he was devoted.

We are to live with an "undivided devotion to the Lord." And if we should die before our Lord returns, before the second coming, let us be found with head cradled in hand, kneeling as if in prayer.

Amen.

Epiphany 4
1 Corinthians 8:1-13

I Hope It Helped

Now concerning food sacrificed to idols: we know that "all of us possess knowledge." Knowledge puffs up, but love builds up. Anyone who claims to know something does not yet have the necessary knowledge; but anyone who loves God is known by him. Hence, as to the eating of food offered to idols, we know that "no idol in the world really exists," and that "there is no God but one." Indeed, even though there may be so-called gods in heaven or on earth — as in fact there are many gods and many lords — yet for us there is one God, the Father, from whom are all things and for whom we exist, and one Lord, Jesus Christ, through whom are all things and through whom we exist. It is not everyone, however, who has this knowledge. Since some have become so accustomed to idols until now, they still think of the food they eat as food offered to an idol; and their conscience, being weak, is defiled. "Food will not bring us close to God." We are no worse off if we do not eat, and no better off if we do. But take care that this liberty of yours does not somehow become a stumbling block to the weak. For if others see you, who possess knowledge, eating in the temple of an idol, might they not, since their conscience is weak, be encouraged to the point of eating food sacrificed to idols? So by your knowledge those weak believers for whom Christ died are destroyed. But when you thus sin against members of your family, and wound their conscience when it is weak, you sin against Christ. Therefore, if food is a cause of their falling, I will never eat meat, so that I may not cause one of them to fall.
1 Corinthians 8:1-13

Samuel Langhorn Clemons is better known to us by his pen name Mark Twain. Four years after his birth, in 1839, his family moved to Hannibal, Missouri, a thriving port city. It was from this locale along the banks of the Mississippi River that Clemons became enamored with the mighty river and the steamboats that traveled to and fro. At the age of seventeen he left home for St. Louis to work as a newspaper reporter. However, the siren call of the river never parted from his ears. Pursuing his passion he secured his river pilot's license in 1858. With the outbreak of the Civil War river trade was no longer profitable, and Clemons returned to his other ambition, which was writing.

Clemons wrote a humorous travel story and elected to sign his name to the article as Mark Twain, the name under which he wrote thereafter. Mark Twain was adopted from a term frequently used and heard by riverboat captains. The minimum depth of the water needed for a boat to pass unobstructed was twelve feet, or two fathoms. "Twain" was slang for two. "Mark" referred that the depth had been measured. When the helmsman heard the cry "Mark Twain" he knew the river passage was safe for further navigation.

As many of us have read the books by Samuel Clemons, we are more familiar with the name on the cover page of Mark Twain. The pen name of Mark Twain is most appropriate because the books are equally as lighthearted as they are challenging, causing one to think and question preconceived notions. The stories provide for us direction, allowing us to navigate the river of life.

Paul in our lectionary reading for this morning was trying to provide instructions for the Christians who were attending church in Corinth. Paul offered the parishioners advice on how to navigate through the disputes that were plaguing the congregation. In his letter, Paul addressed many of the problems that the Corinthians were confronting. In our lesson this morning Paul was centering on dietary laws.

Corinth was a metropolitan port city. Because it was such a cosmopolitan city, many different ethnic groups resided there. With this diversity of population also came the worship of many foreign gods. Some of these gods required food sacrifices as burnt offerings. The food from these rituals would then be served at banquets. Some Christians, when invited to a banquet, felt it was okay to eat the meat. This was because they did not believe in the foreign god and realized that the foreign deity had no power or persuasion over them. Other Christians felt differently. They believed that eating the meat offered to false gods would disturb their spiritual foundation. Paul realized he needed to bring clarity to this contentious environment.

Paul wrote, in essence, that if you could eat the meat offered to a foreign god and not be disturbed by it, that it was permissible to do so. But, if attending that banquet and eating that burnt offering weakened the faith of another Christian, then you really ought to refrain from participating.

The central theme in Paul's discourse is summed up in this single line, "Knowledge puffs up, but love builds up." The issue for us in this congregation today does not involve food offered to false gods; but, it does revolve around confusion. To put it bluntly, not everyone seated in this sanctuary thinks the same way regarding the mandates of being a Christian. We could perhaps place people into groups of like-mindedness, but there would be a disparity of opinions among the groups.

It would be impossible to reconcile all the differing positions, and we couldn't even if we tried. And the question is, should we even try? If we are willing, absent of confrontation, to listen to an opposing point of view perhaps we can be enlightened.

George H. W. Bush, our forty-first president who served from 1989 to 1993, once humorously said, "I have opinions of my own — strong opinions — but I don't always agree with them." We all have strong opinions, especially when it comes to religion, but it would be spiritually healthy for us to entertain the opinions of others.

Immanuel Kant was born on April 22, 1724, in Prussia. Both of his parents were devout followers of Pietism. Pietism believed in intellectualism and having a personal religious experience. Therefore, Bible study was central to their faith.

In 1740, Kant enrolled at the University of Konigsberg as a theology student, but was soon attracted to mathematics and physics. In 1755, he received his doctorate in philosophy and became one of history's most influential writers and teachers on the importance of logic.

In 1781, toward the end of his life, Immanuel Kant published the *Critique of Pure Reason*. It was an enormous book and one of the most influential books on Western thought. In this publication, Kant attempted to explain how reason and experiences interact with thought and understanding. In his concluding section of *Critique of Pure Reason*, Kant argued that all philosophy ultimately aims at answering these three questions: "What can I know? What should I do? What may I hope?"

The three questions posed by Immanuel Kant are probably the same three questions we keep asking about Christianity: "What can I know? What should I do? What may I hope?"

"What can I know?" The answer is probably very little. Miracles, the virgin birth, the resurrection, the meaning of heaven, the form in which God takes, how can a loving God allow evil, the origins of creation, and countless other questions will always remain a mystery. They are unanswerable. It is by faith that we believe and continue with our questions, our uncertainties.

"What should I do?" This question is a little easier. It means I continue to live by faith. It means I continue to live a life that is representative of the Sermon on the Mount. It means I strive to live a life that demonstrates to others that I am a disciple of Jesus.

"What may I hope?" I guess I can hope that my life is an example of Jesus and will make the world a better place. I guess I can hope that my life will be a blessing to other individuals. I can hope that I will not disturb or detract from the faith of another Christian.

"What can I know? What should I do? What may I hope?" Perhaps these can be best answered by returning to the words of Paul, that, "Knowledge puffs up, but love builds up." Knowledge — we will never know everything that we would like to know. Love — we will always be able to enrich the life of others.

Danny Kaye was an American actor, singer, dancer, comedian, and musician. He was in seventeen movies, for which he was most noted for his physical comedy and singing. In 1954, Kaye was the ambassador-at-large for UNICEF. Kaye died in 1987, at the age of 76, from hepatitis C, that he caught from a blood transfusion during heart surgery. Danny Kaye was always regarded as a good, jovial, and happy person. Kaye once said, "Life is a great big canvas, and you should throw all the paint you can on it."

What can I know? What should I do? What may I hope? Perhaps the answer is to throw all the paint that we can on the canvas of life. Brilliant colors, vibrant colors, rousing colors — colors that will restore the lives of individuals who are dejected, disheartened, and depressed. Throw the colors that will revive the lost, the weary, and the forsaken. Paint colors that will instill peace and tranquility into the lives of those who anxious, and afraid, and worried.

Perhaps by painting a canvas with flourishing colors of joy, creating a hue of unity, we will be less concerned by those theological questions that can divide us and stymie us.

Paul Williams and Kenneth Ascher needed to write an opening song for *The Muppet Movie*. They had a discussion about a film they both loved, which was Walt Disney's adaptation of Pinocchio. At the beginning of *Pinocchio*, Jiminy Cricket sings "When You Wish Upon A Star," which the writers felt set the mood for the whole picture.

Kermit the Frog would be in the opening scene of *The Muppet Movie*, and like Jimminy Cricket, Williams and Ascher wanted Kermit to sing a song that would set the mood for the entire film. They had completed the song, but they were unable to find a title for it. The answer came when a friend asked them "What's the problem? You are having difficulty finding that rainbow connection between people and their dreams?" They knew at once that they had their title, "The Rainbow Connection."

As the movie opened, Kermit was sitting in a swamp pondering the big questions of life. Then Kermit sees a rainbow reflected in the still water and the answers came to him. Williams later recalled, "The amazing thing about the song is that it's a song about questions instead of answers...The song addressed that inner voice that told Kermit he could try to do those big things." The song is about hope and optimism and blind faith and love.

The song reached #25 on Billboard's "Hot 100 Singles" chart in 1979 and the American Film Institute named "The Rainbow Connection" the number 74 of the greatest movie songs of all time. The song begins with lyrics that ask questions concerning the reason so many songs contain lyrics about rainbows. It goes on to say there is a connection between lovers, dreamers, rainbows, and himself. You may wish to pull the lyrics up from the internet and read them for yourself.

At the end of the song Kermit admits that hearing about it — that connection made him feel it was something he was supposed to be — connected.

We are all a part of the rainbow connection. As the song "The Rainbow Connection" implores, that *"It's something that I'm supposed to be."* We may have our theological differences, but together we can love and dream. And if we can love together and if we can dream together, then, perhaps someday we'll find that rainbow connection.

John Dominic Crossan is a former Roman Catholic priest. In 1969 he joined the faculty of DePaul University as a New Testament scholar. His books are widely read and discussed today, especially for their emphasis on the humanity of Jesus. Crossan taught that Jesus was a healer and man of great wisdom and courage whose ministry was one of inclusiveness, tolerance, and liberation. Crossan said that Jesus' "strategy was the combination of free healing and common eating that negated the hierarchical and patronal normalcies of Jewish religion and Roman power."

Crossan contended that the unnamed woman was possibly the first Christian. In Matthew's gospel we read of her story: "While Jesus was in Bethany in the home of Simon the Leper, a woman came to him with an alabaster jar of very expensive perfume, which she poured on his head as he was reclining at the table. When the disciples saw this, they were indignant. 'Why this waste?' they asked. 'This perfume could have been sold at a high price and the money given to the poor.' Aware of this, Jesus said to them, 'Why are you bothering this woman? She has done a beautiful thing to me.'"

In Crossan's estimation only this unnamed woman understood, at this point in the ministry of Jesus, that Jesus was going to be crucified for our sins. With this understanding, by anointing his head with oil, she was preparing Jesus for burial. While the other disciples should have been knowledgeable of this, they were instead arguing amongst themselves. The unnamed woman, who should not have understood, did understand, and was building up in love.

As Paul wrote, "Knowledge puffs up, but love builds up."

Love has always been the foundation of the church. Love will always be the foundation of the church. Knowledge is important, but it will always take second place to love. We should be knowledgeable and informed Christians, but it is even more important that we are loving, gentle, considerate, and caring Christians. We may not always see eye-to-eye with our neighbor in the pew; but, we can always see heart-to-heart.

John D. Rockefeller, Jr. believed in the United Nations. He also thought it was not proper for such a distinguished and important agency to be meeting in a skating rink in Queens. He was so disturbed when no site could be located to build the needed structure, that he took it upon himself to locate the perfect place for the headquarters of the world's institution for peace. He searched for property coast to coast, but his secret desire was to have the United Nations in New York City.

Unable to locate any suitable property on Manhattan or elsewhere, he called a family conference. The Rockefeller family decided to donate 2,000 acres of their own land in Westchester County. Plans for the new building were about to commence when Rockefeller balked on his offer, still believing the United Nations should be in New York City.

Once again, he searched the map for an appropriate site. He discovered a place along the East River that would be excellent, but it was a property on which William Zeckendorf planned to build his $150 million "Dream City." Three hours later, Rockefeller arrived unannounced at Zeckendorf's wedding reception. He arrived toting a map of the city. After a short conversation, he convinced Zeckendorf to sell the land for $8.5 million, which Rockefeller paid for himself. The next day Rockefeller's son, Nelson, delivered the seventeen-acre gift to the United Nations Site Committee. The only comment that the elder Rockefeller would make regarding his gift was: "I hope it helped."

Let us employ ourselves in such a way that we are able to say, "I hope it helped."

Amen.

Epiphany 5
1 Corinthians 9:16-23

140 or 300,000

If I proclaim the gospel, this gives me no ground for boasting, for an obligation is laid on me, and woe to me if I do not proclaim the gospel! For if I do this of my own will, I have a reward; but if not of my own will, I am entrusted with a commission. What then is my reward? Just this: that in my proclamation I may make the gospel free of charge, so as not to make full use of my rights in the gospel. For though I am free with respect to all, I have made myself a slave to all, so that I might win more of them. To the Jews I became as a Jew, in order to win Jews. To those under the law I became as one under the law (though I myself am not under the law) so that I might win those under the law. To those outside the law I became as one outside the law (though I am not free from God's law but am under Christ's law) so that I might win those outside the law. To the weak I became weak, so that I might win the weak. I have become all things to all people, that I might by all means save some. I do it all for the sake of the gospel, so that I may share in its blessings.
1 Corinthians 9:16-23

Jimmy Carter was asked to speak to a church in the small town of Preston, Georgia. The church was holding a week of revival meetings, and the topic assigned to Carter was "Christian Witnessing." As Carter sat in the front room of his home preparing his speech, he had a sense of self-satisfaction. Undoubtedly, Carter thought, the invitation from the Preston congregation came because they had heard of the wonderful evangelical work he had done for his home church in Plains.

As Carter was composing his speech, he decided that he would make an impression on the Preston congregation by sharing how many home visits he made in Plains on behalf of God. Carter then began to calculate how many individuals he had witnessed to. It had now been fourteen years since he returned home to Plains since serving in the Navy. As a deacon in the church, he made it a point to visit two families each year. Carter, along with another deacon, would read to the family from the Bible, share the events occurring at the church, briefly share their religious beliefs, small talk about community events, then they would have a prayer and depart. Carter decided to assign an average of five people to each home. In his notes, he proudly put the figure of 140 people to whom he had witnessed .

As Carter was looking at the figure and congratulating himself, he recalled the 1966 governor's election. Having entered the race late, Carter had to abandon everything to campaign. Carter surrendered everything that he cared about — his family, his farm, his bird dogs — in order to campaign sixteen to eighteen hours each day, trying to personally greet as many Georgia voters as possible. At the end of the almost-successful campaign, Carter met more than 300,000 voters.

Jimmy Carter, in his autobiography *Why Not The Best?,* then wrote this line of self-condemnation. Carter wrote, "The comparison struck me — 300,000 visits for myself in three months, and 140 visits for God in fourteen years!"

With that realization, Carter wrote, "I began to read the Bible with a new interest and perspective, and to understand more clearly the admonitions about pride and self-satisfaction." Jimmy Carter realized he was a self-righteous Pharisee. With that realization, Carter wrote, I began "to search more diligently for a closer personal relationship with God among my different business, professional and political interests."

We are called to be evangelists. We are called to share with others the message of salvation. We are called to witness to others about how Jesus Christ can transform lives. Like Jimmy Carter, we are probably self-righteous enough to congratulate ourselves for doing a better job than we really are.

Do we have enough fingers and toes to count the number of individuals to whom we have witnessed?

In witnessing I am not referring to that casual mention of the name of Jesus if it naturally occurs in the course of a conversation. What I am referring to is that deliberate and forthright introduction of Jesus Christ to another individual. What is the sum total of your calculations — 140 or 300,000?

In our lectionary reading for this morning Paul describes his approach to evangelism. And we can use Paul's method as an outline for our own personal approach. I say our own personal approach for each of us is different, so how we witness must be compatible to our individual personalities.

I am speaking of an approach, not an avoidance to evangelism. We will not read anywhere in Paul's writings where it is acceptable to say: I won't, I can't, I'm too shy, I don't know anyone, I wouldn't know what to say, I'm never presented with an opportunity. If these reasons, or would it be proper to call them excuses, are acceptable then the church would never have grown beyond the original twelve gathered in the Upper Room.

To say we have excuses not to witness for Jesus is a harsh word, but it is probably a correct and accurate word to use. It is because we do know people who need to hear the message of the scriptures. It is because we do know more about the Bible and religion than we are willing to admit. It is because daily living abounds with opportunities. It is because the boldness of the gospel message transcends meekness.

We should follow the example of Paul who wrote that "an obligation is laid on me, and woe to me if I do not proclaim the gospel!" Paul realized that witnessing was not an option, but it was a mandate. Paul realized that witnessing was not something he could accept or reject on a whim, but it was a requirement. Paul realized that witnessing was not something one volunteered to do, but it was something one was called to do. And woe to us if we do not accept that mandate, that requirement, that calling.

Don Carlos De Seso was an Italian who served in the court of the Spanish King Philip II. De Seso's imperial duties allowed him to travel extensively across the continent. In the course of his travels he was introduced to Lutheranism, and how those Protestant teachings differed from those of Roman Catholic Spain. On his return to Spain, De Seso led hundreds into the new faith of the Protestant Reformation. King Philip and Pope Paul IV refused to allow a Protestant witness in Spain. Because of his preaching, De Seso was condemned as a heretic.

On October 8, 1559, the Spanish Inquisition held a great *auto da fe*, which literally means "act of faith." It is a public ceremony when heretics are paraded, sentenced, and then executed. When De Seso was led past King Philip to be burned at the stake, De Seso said, "Is it thus that you allow innocent subjects to be persecuted?" Philip's response was, "If it were my own son, I would fetch the wood to burn him, were he such a wretch as you are!"

Two men had to hold De Seso up, so weak was he from fifteen months of imprisonment and torture. As the flames rose slowly around him, De Seso called upon the soldiers in attendance to heap up more fuel. Watching the bravery of De Seso, Lutheranism continued to spread throughout Spain.

Evangelism is not sitting comfortably on cushioned sanctuary pews; but, evangelism is a willingness to be led to the burning stake. The issue today is not the same as sixteenth century Spain, where two Christian denominations were in opposition to one another.

But, for Paul there was an issue between Jews and Christians, and Paul saw it as his mission to convert Jews. It is still the same for us today, and to Paul's list we can add Muslims, Hindus, and Buddhists. As Paul made no apologies, we should make no apology either that Christianity is the healthiest and most meaningful of all religions.

The evangelical issues today still include what it traditionally has always been understood to be, and that is to call unbelievers to repent and be baptized. It is to call the agnostic to once again return to the church. It is to call the disillusioned to once again reaffirm their faith. This is the obligation that is laid upon us and woe to us if we fail to be obedient.

Paul wrote that in accepting the obligation to share the gospel message, he adapted the message for his audience. Paul wrote, "I have made myself a slave to all, so I might win more of them."

Paul wrote, "I have become all things to all people that I might by all means save some." Paul then went on to explain that to the Jews he became a Jew, and to the Gentiles he became a Gentile.

Paul was not implying that he was a hypocrite, who said one thing to one person and something entirely different to another person. What Paul was saying is that he did whatever he could to get along with people, to be accepted by them, so they would listen to his message.

The most effective form of evangelism is called "relational evangelism." Relational evangelism is not confrontational evangelism, but it is interpersonal evangelism. It is sometimes referred to as "friendship evangelism." It is also described as "one-on-one" or "personal" evangelism. Some, who stress the importance of our attitude in these relationships, call it "contagious Christianity," or "lifestyle evangelism."

By whatever title you ascribe to it, the interpretation is the same. It is defined around "earning the right to be heard." Earning the right to be heard means building an intentional relationship, earn credibility, and wait for spiritual conversation to come about. When the topic of faith comes up, you've earned the right to share your faith in Christ. But, we must be cautious that waiting does not become an excuse for not doing. Waiting to be heard still means that we can create some incentives to be heard.

What we do need is a sincere desire. And it is the sincerity of this conviction that motivates us.

When Count Niclaus Ludwig von Zinzendrof, the founder of the Moravians, was ten years old he began to share with his playmates that Jesus was their redeemer. Zinzendrof later reflected on his early attempts at witnessing, surmising, "My deficiency in knowledge was compensated by sincerity." Zinzendrof's deficiency in knowledge was compensated by sincerity is relational evangelism. In testifying for Jesus, the love our words express will surmount any limitations of elocution and knowledge we may impose upon ourselves as a hindrance.

Relational evangelism is found throughout the New Testament as an effective means to win converts. Andrew brought his brother Peter to Jesus. Philip brought his friend Nathanael. The Samaritan woman told her whole town about her encounter with

Jesus. The exorcised man from the Gerasenes went home and told his friends how much Jesus had done for him. Matthew invited his friends to a dinner party where they could meet Jesus. Zacchaeus invited many of his friends to a dinner party. Peter spoke to Cornelius, but the whole household got baptized. Jesus ate with tax collectors and sinners, which was a relational experience.

We are the New Testament of today. We are Andrew, Philip, the Samaritan woman, Matthew, and Zacchaeus who witnessed for Christ. We know the people to whom they witnessed, because all around us we know Nathanael and Cornelius, friends in households and friends in the community. We are without excuse.

Why did Paul witness? Paul said he witnessed for this reason, "I do it for the sake of the gospel, so that I may share in its blessings." Paul did not share the gospel message to receive a monetary reward, but he did it for a spiritual reward. Paul witnessed to others for the joy of knowing he brought joy into their lives. Paul witnessed because of the inner peace he received knowing he brought inner peace and tranquility into the lives of others. Paul did it for he understood the freedom of salvation and he wanted others to experience the freedom of being forgiven of sin.

This is a spiritual blessing that we all should seek. If we truly believe in the transforming power of Jesus Christ, then we should have a real and valid feeling of satisfaction when we know that another individual, because of our personal testimony, has come to know, as Paul wrote in Philippians, and the *New Living Bible* translates as, "Then you will experience God's peace, which exceeds anything we can understand."

A very long and controversial hearing was held in the Senate before Clarence Thomas was approved as a justice for the United States Supreme Court in 1991. Clarence found the process to be disgraceful and insulting. Yet, he persisted because he believed in his own innocence. Bolstered by the Holy Spirit, Clarence remained in the hearings until his Senate confirmation. Each morning during these anguished months, Clarence and his wife Virginia would meet in their home with two other couples, shut the kitchen blinds, play Christian praise music, and pray for two or three hours. It was during these prayer sessions that Thomas gained peace of soul, willing to accept, in Thomas' own words, what was "God's purpose" for him.

Clarence and Virginia Thomas, because they had a personal relationship with Jesus Christ, were able to "experience God's peace, which exceeds anything we can understand." We are evangelists, because we want everyone to experience what Clarence and Virginia have experienced during their time of deepest anguish.

Peter, in his sermon in Jerusalem, introduced it by saying, "Listen to what I say." Listening to the Lord is clearly what Clarence Thomas and his wife Virginia did. The Jewish constituents in Jerusalem were willing to pause long enough to listen to Peter, and in so doing thousands were converted and received the blessing of inner peace.

If we are willing to ask people to "Listen to what I say," if we are willing to witness to the gospel message, then all who hear and come to believe will know both the peace of God and God's purpose for their lives. It is for that reason we accept the obligation to be an evangelist.

Amen.

Transfiguration of Our Lord
2 Corinthians 4:3-6

The Red Coat

And even if our gospel is veiled, it is veiled to those who are perishing. In their case the god of this world has blinded the minds of the unbelievers, to keep them from seeing the light of the gospel of the glory of Christ, who is the image of God. For we do not proclaim ourselves; we proclaim Jesus Christ as Lord and ourselves as your slaves for Jesus' sake. For it is the God who said, "Let light shine out of darkness," who has shone in our hearts to give the light of the knowledge of the glory of God in the face of Jesus Christ.
2 Corinthians 4:3-6

Steven Spielberg's movie *Schindler's List*, which premiered on December 15, 1993, was based on a true story. The movie was about Oskar Schindler, who was a German businessman in Poland during World War II. As a businessman, Schindler saw an opportunity to make money from the Nazis' war machine. Schindler started a company to make cookware and utensils, using bribes to win military contracts. By staffing his plant with Jews from the Krakow's ghetto, Schindler had a dependable unpaid labor force.

However, in 1942, all of Krakow's Jews were assigned to the Plaszow Forced Labor Camp, which was overseen by a commandant who was an embittered alcoholic. The commandant occasionally shot prisoners from his balcony. This was also when Schindler saw many of his Jewish employees being taken to the gas chambers. He suddenly realized he was unwittingly contributing to their deaths. At this point in the movie, Schindler developed a conscience. He realized that his factory, which then manufactured ammunition, was the only thing preventing his Jewish workers from being shipped to the death camps. Soon Schindler demanded more workers and started bribing Nazi leaders to keep Jews on his employee lists and out of the camps.

By the time the camp was liberated by the allies, Schindler had lost his entire fortune. He had used all his money on bribes and employing workers he did not need in order to save 1,100 Jews from death in the gas chambers.

On May 8, 1945, Germany surrendered and the war came to an end. On this day, Schindler gathered all of his workers together on the factory floor and shared the good news. He then asked the Jews not to seek revenge for what had been done to them, and called for a moment of silence in memory of those who had died. He also encouraged the members of the SS who were present to go home peacefully and without further bloodshed.

When the war was over the *Schindlerjuden*, which means "Schindler Jews," as those Jews who were on the work list that spared their lives called themselves, gave Schindler a ring engraved with this verse from the Talmud, "Whoever saves one life saves the world entire." Schindler died in Hildesheim in Germany October 9, 1974. He wanted to be buried in Jerusalem, saying, "My children are here."

Steven Spielberg in his movie, *Schindler's List*, provided a visual representation of evil. Spielberg filmed the movie in black-and-white, which Spielberg considered a representation of the Holocaust. Spielberg said, "The Holocaust was life without light. For me the symbol of life is color. That's why a film about the Holocaust has to be in black-and-white."

What most people who have seen the movie best remember is the little girl in the red coat. She appeared twice in the movie. While the film is shot in black-and-white, the red coat is the only object seen in color. In the scene when the Krakow ghetto was being liquidated, Schindler's attention affixed upon this one girl wearing a red coat. The next time the red coat appeared, Schindler saw the child lying on a cart transporting bodies to the crematorium. Schindler suddenly realized his own contribution to the Holocaust. This was when Schindler realized the evil of the Nazi regime, and began his plans to save the lives of his Jewish workers. Film critics referred to the girl in the red coat as a "marker," used by Spielberg to denote the transformation of Oskar Schindler's change of conscience.

Spielberg said the scene of the little girl in the red coat was intended to symbolize how members of the highest levels of government in the United States knew the Holocaust was occurring, yet did nothing to stop it. Spielberg said, "It was as obvious as a little girl wearing a red coat, walking down the street, and yet nothing was done to bomb the German rail lines. Nothing was being done to slow down ... the annihilation of European Jewry. That was my message in letting that scene be in color."

The girl in the red coat depicted in the film was Roma Ligocka. Ligocka was known among those in the ghetto for her red coat. Unlike Spielberg's child, Ligocka survived the Holocaust and wrote her autobiography titled, *The Girl in the Red Coat: A Memoir*.

The question becomes, "What will it take for us to help someone see the red coat?" Evil... Paul in our lectionary reading for this morning was forthright in saying it was evil that keeps people from believing in the Lord Jesus Christ. Paul wrote, "In their case the god of this world has blinded the minds of the unbelievers." Paul was making a direct reference that "the god of this world" is Satan. That "the god of this world" is the devil.

Paul believed in Satan, and so should we. Paul in many of his letters made references to Satan as the "prince of the power of the air," as "the tempter," as "the evil one," and as "the spirit that is now at work in the sons of disobedience." Paul wrote that Satan "prowls like a roaring lion."

The origin of Satan is uncertain, and there have been many biblical explanations for Satan's creation. But, all the explanations share one common theme, and that is Satan is in a power struggle against God. In that power struggle Satan attempts to win converts to the demonic side of the battle.

In the Old Testament, the Hebrew word for Satan means "adversary." In the New Testament Satan is referred to as "the adversary," as "the false accuser," and as "the slanderer." All of the defining terms have a common thread, and that is Satan wants to deceive us from believing in God.

This is why we should take notice that some early transcripts of the Lord's Prayer translated what we say today "deliver us from evil," as "deliver us from the evil one." We need to pray that we are delivered from the power and ensnarement of Satan.

The early church fathers believed in the power of Satan. One of the best descriptions of Satan is recorded for us in a sermon preached by Origen. Origen was born in the Egyptian city of Alexandria and lived from the year 185 to the year 254. He is considered by some the first theologian of stature in the church. He wrote a sermon on almost every verse in the entire Bible. Origen preached that the Christian life is a struggle against the devil's "fiery darts" and "nets." "Fiery darts" and "nets" is a good description on how the devil tries to entrap us.

In the Creation story the serpent is often equated as being Satan, though that is never specified in the scriptures. Sin came into the world with this single incident. When the serpent said to Eve, "Did God really say, 'You must not eat from any tree in the garden?'" the stage was set. A dialogue ensued in which Satan convinced Eve that she should eat the fruit from the tree of knowledge of good and evil, which tradition holds was an apple. Satan's final convincing argument was, "You will not certainly die. For God knows that when you eat from it your eyes will be opened, and you will be like God, knowing good and evil."

"You will be like God." When Eve, then Adam, questioned God and ate the apple they made themselves like God. This was idolatry. Idolatry is worshiping anything other than God. Adam and Eve were not content to take God for his word, they had to know for themselves. The eating of the apple was an act of disobedience and detachment from God. And both Adam and Eve did die, not physically but spiritually.

There is a fruit-filled cornucopia of what it means to be like God today.

There is the fruit of atheism. The word atheism means "without God." The atheist is the person who says that there is no God. Carl Sagan was one of the world's most famous atheists. Sagan was an astronomer who narrated and co-wrote the award-winning 1980 television series *Cosmos: A Personal Voyage*. *Cosmos* was the most widely watched series in the history of American public television. The program has been seen by at least 500 million people across sixty different countries. Sagan summed up atheism when he declared, "The Cosmos is all that is or ever was or ever will be." Isaac Asimov, another famous atheist, was a prolific writer. He wrote or edited more than 500 books and an estimated 90,000 letters and postcards. Asimov wrote science fiction and, along with Robert A. Heinlein and Arthur C. Clarke, he was considered one of the "Big Three" science fiction writers during the twentieth century. Asimov once said, "Emotionally, I am an atheist. I don't have the evidence to prove that God doesn't exist, but I so strongly suspect he doesn't that I don't want to waste my time." An atheist is unable to find any evidence for God's existence; therefore, God does not exist.

There is the fruit of agnostics. The word agnostic means "without knowledge." The agnostic does not boldly proclaim that God does not exist; instead, the agnostic suggests no one can know whether or not God exists because there simply is not enough evidence upon which to base a conclusion. Charles Darwin was an agnostic. Darwin is best known for his development of the theory of evolution which he presented in his 1859 book *On the Origin of Species*. Darwin said, "The mystery of the beginning of all things is insoluble by us; and I for one must be content to remain an agnostic." Clarence Darrow was an agnostic. Darrow was a famous lawyer, who may be best known to us for defending and John T. Scopes, an advocate of evolution, in the Scopes "Monkey" Trial of 1925 in Dayton, Tennessee. Darwin said, "I am an agnostic; I do not pretend to know what many ignorant men are sure of." The agnostic lives in the arena of uncertainty and disbelief.

There is the fruit of the skeptic. A skeptic is a person who habitually doubts the authenticity of accepted beliefs. In particular, a skeptic is a person who doubts the truth of religion, especially Christianity. Thomas Paine was one of the founding fathers of our nation. The many pamphlets he wrote were publicly acknowledged for their reasoned approach to secure colonial freedom from British dominance. In 1793, in the book titled *Age of Reason,* Paine wrote about his skepticism regarding Christianity. Paine wrote, "Whenever we read the obscene stories, the voluptuous debaucheries, the cruel and torturous executions, the unrelenting vindictiveness with which more than half the Bible is filled, it would be more consistent that we called it the word of a demon than the word of God. It is a history of wickedness that has served to corrupt and brutalize mankind…" *The Age of Reason* also attacks

Christianity as a system of superstition that "produces fanatics." When the book reached England, several book sellers were convicted of blasphemy and jailed. Paine was also quoted as saying, "All national institutions of churches, whether Jewish, Christian, or Turkish appear to me no other than human inventions, set up to terrify and enslave mankind, and monopolize power and profit." The skeptic is not prepared to accept anything except that which can be verified empirically, that is by using the five senses. To the skeptic, then, science becomes the only valid method of proving anything. Since God cannot be seen, tasted, heard, touched, or smelled, then skeptics say that either God does not exist or that God cannot be very important even if he does exist.

This is the same environment into which Paul was drawn and into which we are drawn today. It is an environment in which individuals are blind to the existence of God. It is because they can't believe, don't want to believe, or can't be bothered to believe that they do not believe. To get these people to believe, to see the red coat, to have a change in conscience, is a monumental evangelical task.

The task for us, according to Paul, as he wrote in our lectionary reading, "For God, who said, 'Let light shine out of darkness,' made his light shine in our hearts to give us the light of the knowledge of God's glory displayed in the face of Christ." It is our task to bring people out of their darkness of unbelief into the light of belief. We are to be like the prophet Isaiah who said, "The people walking in darkness have seen a great light."

You are up to the challenge. The question is will you accept the challenge? The only guidance you need to bring someone out of darkness and into the light of Christ is a sincere faith and a sincere desire to share that faith. You do not need to be a biblical scholar. You do not need to be a theologian. You don't have to have answers for all the questions. What you need to be able to do is genuinely express what Jesus means to you. What you do need to be able to do with wholeheartedness is share how Jesus brought you out of darkness into the light.

Ernest Borgnine was an American film, television, character, and voice actor whose career spanned more than six decades. He is probably best known to many for his title role in the 1960s sitcom, "McHale's Navy." In filming the movie *Jesus of Nazerath*, Borgnine played the role of the centurion who stood at the foot of the cross, looking up into the face of the crucified Jesus of Nazareth. Since this was a movie, actors only came on the set when needed so, instead of having the actor portraying Jesus, Borgnine stared at an "X" chalk mark where Jesus would have been on the cross. In such a sterile setting, Borgnine had a difficult time capturing the emotions that the Roman soldier must have experienced at that tragic moment. In order to feel the part, Borgnine asked someone to read Luke's account of the crucifixion. As the words were being read, Borgnine felt more and more uncomfortable, ashamed that like the first centurion he failed to acknowledge the Son of God in his own life. Then something miraculous happened — the chalk mark suddenly was transformed into the face of Jesus, lifelike and clear. Captivated by the revelation, Borgnine realized how the centurion who first stood at the foot of the cross must have been affected; in all sincerity, he repeated the soldier's words: "Certainly this man was innocent!" Ernest Borgnine had gone from darkness into the great light. Ernest Borgnine was converted to Christianity.

It is time for us to share the gospel message so unbelievers can have a change in conscience. It is time for us to help people see the red coat. It is time for us to "let light shine out of darkness."

Amen.

www.ingramcontent.com/pod-product-compliance
Lightning Source LLC
Chambersburg PA
CBHW071733040426
42446CB00012B/2344